ONLY A PRAYER AWAY

Only a Prayer Away

Finding Deeper Intimacy with God

John Guest

VINE
BOOKS

Servant Publications
Ann Arbor, Michigan

Copyright © 1985 by John Guest

Cover photo by Ed Cooper
Cover design by John B. Leidy

Published by Servant Publications, Box 8617,
Ann Arbor, Michigan 48107

Vine Books is an imprint of Servant Publications
designed to serve Evangelical Christians

ISBN 0-89283-273-8
Printed in the United States of America
    86 87 88 89 10 9 8 7 6 5 4 3 2

Library of Congress Cataloging in Publication Data

Guest, John 1936—
    Only a prayer away.

    1. Prayer. I. Title.
BV215.G84 1985   248.3'2   85-14617
ISBN 0-89283-273-8

To "Vic" (The Rev. Kenneth H. Druitt),
my father in the faith and pastor for the
first years of my "new life in Christ." His
example gave me the courage to "Preach
the Word (and to) be urgent in season and
out of season. . . ." II Timothy 4:2

Contents

Foreword / 9
  by R. C. Sproul
Introduction / 13

Part I · The Power of Prayer
  1. Walking on the Water / 17
  2. Prayer Changes History / 23
  3. Prayer Changes Us / 29
  4. Prayer Alone Will Suffice / 33

Part II · Teach Us to Pray
  5. Model Prayer / 39
  6. Intimacy and Adoration / 43
  7. Under God's Reign / 47
  8. The Great Secret / 51
  9. The Miracle Cure / 55
  10. Trial and Error / 61
  11. The Devil: His Style Is Wile / 65
  12. Glory, Glory, Hallelujah! / 69

Part III · Principles of Prayer
  13. An Intimate Relationship / 75
  14. An Encompassing Relationship / 79
  15. A Constant Relationship / 83
  16. Boldness in Prayer / 87
  17. An Open Ear / 91
  18. Humbleness Leads to Prayer / 97

Part IV · The Practice of Prayer
  19. Alone with God / 103

20. No Pain, No Gain / 107
21. The Eye of Faith / 111

Part V · Overcoming Doubt in Prayer
22. Doubt, Disobedience, and
    Doublemindedness / 119
23. Walk in the Light / 123
24. Ignorance Is Not Bliss / 127
25. Jesus Understands Suffering / 133
26. An Everlasting Memorial / 137
27. Risking All / 141
28. Yes, No, Wait, Grow / 145

Foreword

by R.C. Sproul

THERE IS AN ACUTE DIFFERENCE between knowing about God and knowing God. There is a profound difference between believing in God and believing God. One involves the brain only; the other requires a commitment of the soul.

We speak of God as the Immortal, Invisible, Only-Wise God. This string of attributes gives some comfort and no small amount of dismay. That God is immortal makes me glad. It means simply that He cannot and therefore will never die. I need not worry that He will ever wear out or be replaced. His throne is established forever. He reigns eternally in His omnipotence. That is good news for a perishing humanity. I rejoice also that He is All-Wise. This sets Him apart from every man. It was Aristotle who taught that in the brain of every wise man could be found the corner of the fool. There is no foolish corner in the mind of God. I find solace in the certain truth that the One who rules the affairs of the universe is not given to blunders or lapses into incompetency. The Peter Principle is arrested at the zenith of human endeavors. It does not extend beyond the apex of the human pyramid.

I rejoice in God's wisdom and in His everlasting power. It is His persistent invisibility that saddens me. Even Hollywood could make the invisible man visible by applying flour to his unseen features. But Pillsbury's best cannot bring God within my vision.

It is difficult for sensual creatures to enjoy fellowship with One who cannot be seen, heard, tasted, touched, or smelled. God remains beyond my senses. How then, can I ever relate to

Him with intimacy? My heart longs for fellowship with Him. I long to hear His voice as the sound of many waters and to catch one glimpse of His refulgent glory.

As a college student I took a course in classical hymnology. Our professor was a sophisticated sort who ridiculed the maudlin hymns that have crept into popular usage. We shared his cynicism toward such songs as "In The Garden" with lyrics like "He walks with me and He Talks with me, and He tells me I am His own."

Such verse seems tawdry. But I cannot deny that in the simplest of terms they express the longing of my heart. Oh, to walk with Him, and to talk with Him. I would crawl over glass to hear audible words from heaven saying to me, "R.C., you are my own."

What I crave is a relationship with God that is both intimate and personal. The great barrier to intimacy is God's invisibility. Because I cannot see Him I tend to doubt His presence. But He is there and promises communion and fellowship with Him. The tool He provides to overcome the barriers is the tool of prayer.

Prayer offers us a link to intimate fellowship with God. Here is where we find what the saints call "mystic sweet communion." One need not be a mystic to enjoy this sweet communion. Prayer is access to God. He hears what I say to Him in prayer. He responds. Not audibly or with a vision of Himself. But His response is real and encourages more prayer. The sweetness of prayer is found in adoration. When we move beyond speaking our requests or placing our petitions before Him we enter into the vail of sweet communion. It is when we praise Him that we bask in His glory.

John Guest understands all that. I have known John for two decades. He is my friend. He is a co-laborer. I love to be with him, especially when I grow stale. He is a mature man, the Rector of St. Stephen's Episcopal Church in Sewickley, Pennsylvania. He is an able man. But what strikes me most about John Guest is that he has never lost the joy of his salvation. He is as excited about Christ today as he was the day he was converted.

When John Guest was converted to Christ he ran home skipping over fire hydrants and clicking his heels in the air. That same electric excitement is still with him. Especially when he preaches... or when he prays. I love to hear him preach and I love to hear him pray. Listening to him pray is like eavesdropping on someone's sweet communion with God.

This book is written by a man of prayer. We can all learn from it.

R.C. Sproul
Spring, 1985

Introduction

THE RECURRING THEME of this book is that prayer expresses the personal privilege of an intimate relationship with God. It does not pretend to be an exhaustive treatment of this privilege, but shares practical wisdom and spiritual insight drawn from the scriptures and thirty years of living in a personal relationship with the Lord Jesus Christ.

In terms of practical wisdom, it has been a joy to put in writing the many helpful tips I have discovered on how to make prayer a part of the "ordinary" Christian's life—to take prayer out of the realm of "monastic piety" or "super-spirituality" and see it as an "everyday" extension of our relationship to God.

The first followers of Jesus made this request, "Teach us to pray." We join with them in sitting at his feet, to learn from what he had to say, and the example he set before them.

I am deeply grateful to John Blattner for his help throughout this project.

Part I

The Power of Prayer

ONE

Walking on the Water

He went up on the mountain to pray. (Mk 6:46)

JESUS HAD JUST COME from performing one of the most magnificent miracles of his ministry, the feeding of the five thousand. He sent his disciples on ahead of him to the other side of the Sea of Galilee, Mark tells us, while he stayed behind to dismiss the crowd. And then, "when evening came, he went up on the mountain to pray"(Mk 6:46).

It was from this elevated place of prayer that he saw the disciples "were making headway painfully, for the wind was against them" (6:48). The day was drawing to a close and nightfall was at hand, but Jesus made no move to assist them. Not until "about the fourth watch of the night" did he come to them, walking on the water.

In those days people divided the night into four "watches," three-hour periods, which began at six in the evening, and went until six in the morning. The beginning of the fourth watch would thus have been about three o'clock in the morning.

Plainly, Jesus had remained at prayer for some considerable time before coming to the disciples' aid. Though he had known of their difficulty for several hours, he chose to spend time with his Father in prayer rather than rush immediately to their rescue.

Jesus' response to the disciples' plight is a model for our response to the pressures, immediacies, and demands of the fast moving society in which we live.

Note that he has already demonstrated the importance of getting involved in meeting the needs of a hurting world. More than any of the other gospel writers, Mark portrays a desperately needy world constantly clamoring after Jesus. In chapter 5, after Jesus has dramatically delivered a man from demonic oppression, he crosses to the other side of the Sea of Galilee, where "a great crowd gathered about him"(5:21). Among the crowd is Jairus, who begs Jesus to come and heal his daughter; as Jesus goes with him, "a great crowd followed him and thronged about him"(5:24); in that crowd was a woman pressing through the crush just to "touch even his garments"(5:28).

In chapter 6 Jesus tries to steal a few quiet moments away from the crowds. "Come away to a lonely place, and rest a while," he says to his disciples, because "they had no leisure even to eat"(6:31). But it was no use. The crowds guess where he is going, and when Jesus arrives at what he supposed was a place of quiet isolation, they are there to greet him.

But instead of being frustrated or angry, Jesus "had compassion on them"(6:34). He taught them and fed them, miraculously, from five loaves and two fish. Only then did he send his disciples on ahead, dismiss the crowds, and go up on the mountainside to pray. And prayer is what he chose even when he saw his disciples struggling to cross the water in the high winds. He delayed several hours before coming to their rescue.

Jesus' world was filled with deeply needy people who persistently clamored for his attention. Your world, and mine, is no different. We are everywhere surrounded by needy people clamoring for *our* assistance. There are people where you work, or where you go to school, or in your neighborhood, who are burdened and in need. You know who they are. There is the friend who is an alcoholic; the associate at work whose marriage is in trouble; the neighbor who has just lost his job; the best friend whose son is on drugs. Then there is your own mother whose health is failing, and your own children who demand all your emotional resources.

What is our reaction to all these needs? Some of us are incredibly over involved. For many of us, the natural reaction is to avoid involvement. After all, we suffer from some of the same problems and needs ourselves. Who are we to get involved? Our own marriage isn't perfect, our own children in trouble, our own health in jeopardy. And so we shrink back into the isolation of our own manageable world.

But Jesus never shrank back. Jesus, when he saw the pain of others, didn't just hide in the safety and quiet of his own personal comfort. He moved to meet their needs. If we are to be genuine followers of Jesus, if we are to be imitators of Jesus, we cannot simply close our eyes to an ailing world. Despite our own needs, we must "reach out and touch someone" who is crying for help.

This is a frightening thought. How are we to get involved? From where are we to draw the resources? How will we find the time, the energy, the wisdom, the patience, the courage?

The answer is profoundly simple. We will find them the same way Jesus did. "He went up on the mountain to pray." Jesus drew his strength from time spent with his Father in prayer. He drew on the deep well of his heavenly Father's resources.

The priority Jesus places on prayer is unmistakable. He noticed at dusk that his disciples were making headway painfully, but he delayed coming to their aid until well into the middle of the night. Where was he in the meantime, and what was he doing? He was on the mountain, alone with his Father, praying. In his humanity Jesus wore out from the draining demands made upon him. He needed the refreshment of prayer, so he took steps to pray in solitude. He availed himself of his Father's presence in a quiet place before setting out to rescue his disciples.

How high a priority do *we* place on prayer? How well have we learned to draw upon the limitless resources of our heavenly Father as we confront our own needs and respond to the needs of those who clamor for our help? If Jesus needed to get alone in prayer, how much more do we need to do likewise?

Our great excuse, of course, is busyness. We are, without question, a busy people, with many demands on our time, many outside forces pressing upon us. But we must decide to make time for prayer.

Martin Luther once described his own prayer life. "On a typical day," he said, "I am charged with the pastorate of three congregations. I teach regularly at the seminary. I have students living in my house. I am writing three books. Countless people write to me. When I start each day, therefore, I make it a point to spend an hour in prayer with God. But if I have a particularly busy day and am more rushed than usual, I make it a point to spend *two* hours with God before I start the day."

Two hours in prayer! How could I possibly manage that? I have to be at the office by 7:00 A.M.! I have to get the kids dressed and off to school! Where would I find even an hour, let alone two hours?

Relax. We needn't begin with anything so dramatic as a daily two-hour prayer time. But we must begin somewhere. Fifteen minutes a day—or even ten minutes—is well within our reach, and will be the beginning of a radical difference in our lives. For once we begin the habit of ten minutes with God, it will be like a certain brand of potato chip—we will just have to have more.

We know all too well how many and how great are the needs that demand our attention. But our prior need is to spend time with God away from the distractions and pain of a voracious world.

Heavenly Father, forgive us for spending so little time with you. Help us to see our need for prayer. By the power of your Spirit, help us to enter into regular times of intimacy with you. Grant that our lives, and the lives of our families and friends, may be transformed because we have met with you.

For reflection and discussion:

—What are some of the needs and problems of those around me in which I could involve myself by praying for them?

—How much time do I regularly set aside to be alone with God in prayer? How much time am I *willing* to spend with him?

TWO

Prayer Changes History

The prayer of a righteous man has great power in its effects.
(Jas 5:16)

IN THE EIGHTEENTH CHAPTER of Luke's Gospel, Jesus tells the story of the widow and the judge. The widow was seeking vindication against an adversary and the judge, for some reason, was not responding to her. But the widow persisted, and eventually the judge gave in and granted her request, lest he be worn out "by her continual coming" (Lk 18:1-8).

The purpose of the parable, Luke says, was to teach the disciples "that they ought always to pray and not lose heart." Other translations read, "to pray and not faint." In other words, the antidote to spiritual discouragement and weariness is prayer. When testing circumstances bear in upon us, we can either lose heart or we can go to God in prayer.

In his first letter to the Thessalonians, Paul urges us to "pray constantly," or to pray "without ceasing"(1 Thes 5:17). Some Christians in past eras have taken that word literally and developed techniques for maintaining a continual state of prayer, so that there is no waking moment in which they are not, in some actual and active sense, praying.

Not everyone interprets the passage in that way, and I am not urging that particular kind of "constant prayer" upon you. But we are nevertheless to be people whose life is marked by ongoing prayer and by continuing fellowship with God. We can and should be people who, in the more colloquial sense, "pray all the time," who "never stop praying."

And for good reason. James assures us that "the prayer of a righteous man"—that is, of a person in right relationship with God—"is powerful in its effects" (Jas 5:16). Things happen when we pray. The history of nations and peoples has been changed because someone prayed.

Remember the story of Sodom and Gomorrah. God deliberately chose to tell Abraham about his plans to destroy the two cities. Armed with this information, Abraham took the opportunity, through prayer, to play a role in the unfolding of God's plan.

Abraham, of course, thought immediately of the fact that his kinsman Lot had settled his family in Sodom. Abraham knew of the wickedness of the inhabitants of Sodom and Gomorrah, but he also knew of the uprightness of Lot, and of the mercy and justice of God. Surely God would not slay the innocent along with the guilty?

> Then Abraham drew near, and said, "Wilt thou indeed destroy the righteous with the wicked? Suppose there are fifty righteous within the city; wilt thou then destroy the place and not spare it for the fifty righteous who are in it? Far be it from thee to do such a thing, to slay the righteous with the wicked, so that the righteous fare as the wicked! Far be that from thee! Shall not the Judge of all the earth do right?" (Gn 18:23-25)

God agreed to spare the cities if fifty righteous people could be found in them. But there were not fifty. Abraham prayed again: would God spare the cities for the sake of forty-five righteous? Yes, but there were not forty-five righteous to be found. Again and again Abraham prayed. Would God spare the cities for the sake of forty righteous people? Thirty? Twenty? Ten?

Because of Abraham's prayer, God was willing to relent from his plans and spare the evil cities for the sake of only ten righteous men. But not even ten could be found. Nevertheless, Abraham's prayers availed for his kinsman Lot and Lot's family. God sent two angels to Lot, to warn him of the impending doom of Sodom and Gomorrah and to enable them to escape. Abraham's prayer changed the history of Lot and his family.

Hezekiah was king of Judah at the time of the invasion of Sennacherib, the fearsome warrior-king of mighty Assyria. Both Hezekiah and the people of Judah deserved the cruel fate Sennacherib intended for them, and Hezekiah knew it. Even so, he prayed and asked God to spare him and his people.

God granted Hezekiah's request. Through the prophet Isaiah, he upbraided Hezekiah and Judah for their short-comings, but he also promised deliverance: "I will defend this city to save it, for my own sake and for the sake of my servant David" (2 Kgs 19:34). Once again, prayer had changed the course of history.

Throughout scripture the pattern is repeated. Elijah prays, and God stops the rain as a sign to King Ahaz. He prays again, and God sends fire from heaven to endorse Elijah's ministry and repudiate the false prophets. Daniel prays, and a remnant is saved to preserve the chosen people through the long captivity in Babylon. Jesus prays, and Lazarus walks out of the tomb alive.

And so it goes, throughout history. The prayer of righteous men and women continues to be powerful in its effects. Mary Queen of Scots once said she feared the prayers of John Knox more than she feared ten thousand armed men. Imagine that: the monarch of a great nation, more fearful of one elderly Scottish minister on his knees than of ten thousand armed soldiers. She understood the power of prayer on the lips of God's people, and was rightly in awe.

One contemporary example: on February 17th, 1985, some four hundred men and women gathered to pray in St. Patrick's

Church, in Canonsburg, Pennsylvania and I had joined them.
The McGraw-Edison Company had told its employees that
without a considerable "giveback" in wages and benefits the
company would close down its Canonsburg plant; the union
leadership had said no. The impact on the town would be
disastrous. But on that fateful day, The Rev. David Kinsey,
chairman of the Canonsburg Ministerial Association, along
with the ministers of the town, labor and management
personnel from McGraw Edison, their families, and a large
ecumenical group of praying people, gathered to ask God to
change hearts and change history.

At the climax of that prayer rally, Wayne T. Alderson, a
Christian labor relations and management consultant and
founder of Value of the Person Inc., called the senior
management representative for McGraw-Edison and the
president of the local United Steel Workers Union to come
and stand with him at the front of the church. What a sight to
behold in the beleaguered town of Canonsburg!

The labor leader prayed for McGraw-Edison management,
and the manager prayed for the trade union leaders and
membership. The result: two days later, management changed
its offer (though there was still to be a reduction in salary and
benefits) and the labor force changed its vote, and praying
people had changed the history of Canonsburg and McGraw-
Edison.

It is the same where you live. The prayer of God's people can
change things. If we will be a people of prayer, as we are called
to be, and will pray fervently and in faith, as we are exhorted to
do, God will change the course of history: the history of our
lives, our families, our cities, our nation. Like Abraham, God
chooses to give us a part in his direction of human events. That
is the privilege of prayer God grants to us.

*Lord, we thank you for your power at work through our prayer.
Stimulate us to remember to pray and not to lose heart. Teach us
to call upon you and see hearts changed, history changed, and the
Lord Jesus glorified.*

For reflection and discussion:

—In what areas of my life am I tempted to grow weary or discouraged? Where is God offering me the opportunity to change circumstances through prayer?

—How can my daily life come to be characterized less by worry and more by prayer?

THREE

Prayer Changes Us

Here am I! Send me. (Is 6:8)

IT IS REMARKABLE TO THINK that God has given us a partnership with him in directing the course of human events. It is extraordinary to realize that our prayer can change events and circumstances in the world around us. But what is just as remarkable is that when we pray, *we* change. More often than not we become the answer to our own prayers as we open up ourselves to God in prayer.

We so easily overlook this! We come to God in prayer detached from the very situation we are praying about, as though we had nothing to do with it. "God, change the situation," we pray, or "Lord, make this difficult relationship work better," or "Jesus, resolve this complicated problem." All the while we fail to take account of the obvious fact that we are part of the awkward situation, the difficult relationship, the complicated problem. If God actually is to change it, will he not begin by changing us and the part we have to play in it? The very fact we are concerned about the problem, and are bringing it before him in prayer, makes us prime candidates to be used by him in solving it!

For instance, the sixth chapter of Isaiah opens with the death of King Uzziah. The year was 740 B.C. History tells that King Uzziah had reigned for some fifty years. Under his leadership the borders of Judah had been secured, the economy expanded, the quality and comfort of life taken for granted. Then he died! The question in every heart and on every lip was, "What next?"

You can be sure that it was concern for the crisis in the government that drove Isaiah to pray. He went to the Temple burdened for his nation. But he came from the Temple with a message for his nation. He went to the Temple to pray and came from the Temple a prophet. He sought God's face on behalf of the people, but he was sent to the people on behalf of God. No doubt his first prayer was "send us help" but his last prayer was "send me."

Nowhere is this principle more applicable than in the area of personal relationships. Nothing can be so irritating a "thorn in the flesh" as a relationship we cannot avoid with a person we cannot stand! It may be a neighbor or a co-worker. It may be a boss. It may even—on a more temporary basis, one hopes—be husband or wife, parent or child. How many times have we come before the Lord, hot and hurt, frustrated and confused, and pleaded with him: "Lord, isn't there anything you can do about this?"

But remember, it takes two. Any troubled relationship involves not only the other person—who so often becomes the exclusive focus of our prayer—but ourselves as well. Even though we may consider them the real problem, it is wonderful how, once we begin to pray, God changes us. Paul told the Romans, "If possible, so far as it depends upon you, live peaceably with all" (Rom 12:18). We are not entirely the cause of every relationship difficulty we experience—but we do have some part in it. Asking God to show us where we are at fault and to change us may not be where the process ends, but marvelously it is where it invariably begins.

A very close friend of mine—indeed, the man for whom I came to Pittsburgh to work—had a dramatic experience of this very phenomenon. Don worked in a large insurance company. His boss in that company was a man he simply couldn't stand.

It got to the point where the boss dominated Don's life because Don hated him so. All Don could think about was how miserable this man was making his life, and about what he was going to say or do the next time he saw him. It was eating him alive, giving him sleepless nights.

Finally Don shared his situation with a friend, the Rev. Sam Shoemaker. "Don, you've got some serious praying to do," Sam told him. "You've got to start praying for this man you find so unbearable." Don's crass response was, "The hell I will!" It went against his very nature, but Don finally accepted the challenge and put prayer into action. He gave it a try.

One day a few months later, as Don was passing his boss's office, the man called him in.

"What is it with you?" the man said in a puzzled voice.

"What do you mean?" asked Don.

"I mean what's happened to you? You've changed!"

It turned out, as it so often does, that the relationship problem which was causing Don such grief, owed as much to Don's attitude as to his boss. How it got started Don could never quite say. But before it could be resolved, a fundamental change had to take place in Don. When Don began to pray earnestly for his boss, it was his own heart that God changed. God's method for resolving the problem invariably is to change the one who prays.

Not all our problems are as extreme as Don's, nor will the answers to them always be so clear-cut and dramatic. But the basic principle is the same: God can change outside circumstances, and he frequently does. But more often than not he changes *us.* And it is through prayer that we put ourselves in position to be changed by him. So, if you have a problem in your marriage, pray about it. If you have problems with your children, pray about them. If you have problems at work, or with other people, bring them to the Lord in prayer. Offer yourself to the Lord as Isaiah did. But watch out! Open yourself to the Lord and he is sure to change you. Instead of being part of the problem you become part of the solution.

Lord Jesus Christ, you have called us to pray. We ask that you would encourage us to be people of prayer, people who pray without ceasing, people who bring all our needs before you, people who bring our very selves before you to be touched and changed by your power.

For reflection and discussion:

—What are the difficult situations in my life that God may want to change by changing me?

—How can I more effectively put myself in position to seek God's direction for my life day by day?

FOUR

Prayer Alone Will Suffice

This kind cannot be driven out by anything but prayer.
(Mk 9:29)

THE LESSON COULD NOT have been driven home more dramatically.

Try to imagine the anguish of the disciples as they confront the terrifying demonic power gripping the young boy who has been brought to them. "Wherever it seizes him," the boy's father explains, "it dashes him down; and he foams and grinds his teeth and becomes rigid . . . it has often cast him into the fire and into the water, to destroy him"(Mk 9:18, 22).

The disciples are no strangers to the power of the evil one as it manifests itself in such unfortunate people. They have seen the spectacular deliverance of the man of the Gerasenes, in whom the demons were so numerous that they named themselves, corporately, "Legion" (Mk 5:1-20). Indeed, by now the casting out of evil spirits has become almost a routine aspect of Jesus' ministry, to which the disciples are routine witnesses (see Mk 1:21-28, 32-34; 3:11-12).

Moreover, they themselves have had a share in this kind of ministry. When the twelve were sent out on their first missionary expedition, they were expressly commissioned with "authority over the unclean spirits." Evidently they learned to wield that authority, for Mark reports that "they cast out many demons, and anointed with oil many that were sick and healed them" (Mk 6:7, 12-13).

But they had not yet encountered a case as terrifying as the one now before them. How long they tried in vain to drive out the evil spirit, we do not know. We *do* know that the father of the possessed boy lost confidence in their efforts. Imagine their frustration and embarrassment when he brought his son to Jesus and explained, "I asked your disciples to cast it out, and they were not able" (Mk 9:18).

Jesus, of course, succeeds where his followers have failed: with a word of command and a touch of healing, he banishes the evil spirit and restores the boy to full health. The chastened disciples wait until Jesus has entered the house, and then ask him privately, "Why could we not cast it out?" (9:28).

His answer is startling. How might we expect Jesus to respond to their question? What reason might we give for his ability to wield authority where their efforts have failed? His omnipotence as the Son of God? A special authority residing in him because of his unique nature?

No. "This kind cannot be driven out by anything but prayer" (9:29). That is all. The disciples' failure stems not from lack of divine prerogatives, but from lack of prayer. Had they prayed more, been more "men of prayer," Jesus seems to suggest (some versions of the account also mention fasting as an important element which gave evidence of sincerity and intensity in prayer) they would have succeeded here as in so many previous instances.

This word of Jesus is both comforting and troubling, and for precisely the same reason: because it locates the effective exercise of spiritual power squarely within the province of each one of us. Our humanity need no longer limit our ability to overcome spiritual opposition: the power of prayer is, after all, available to us. But at the same time, we may no longer hide behind our humanity, no longer use it to excuse our spiritual impotence: the power of prayer is available to us—if only we will learn to take advantage of it.

We must never allow ourselves to lose sight of the spiritual realities that underlie the natural realities around us. We may never find ourselves face to face with a demon-possessed person, as did Jesus. The kinds of problems we typically encounter—marriage problems, work problems, relationship problems, and the rest—seem so mundane, so matter-of-fact, by contrast. But at root they are *spiritual* problems. They must be addressed, not merely in the realm of human wisdom and effort, but also in the realm of the spirit. "For we are not contending against flesh and blood, but against the principalities, against the powers, against the world rulers of this present darkness, against the spiritual hosts of wickedness in the heavenly places" (Eph 6:12).

The difficulties we confront in our lives are simply skirmishes in a larger war, the war between the kingdom of light and the kingdom of darkness. It is a spiritual war, and it must be fought with spiritual weapons: with truth, Paul says, and with righteousness, with the gospel and the shield of faith, with the helmet of salvation and the word of God.

And with prayer. Paul concludes his list of the weapons of spiritual warfare with the exhortation to "pray at all times in the spirit, with all prayer and supplication" (Eph 6:18). Jesus, who understood the problems of human life as spiritual battles, saw that they could be won only by prayer.

When John Wesley led the evangelical awakening in eighteenth-century England, he faced enormous obstacles. The wickedness of life and the pagan elements of popular culture make those of our own day seem pale by comparison. Many of the clergy of the day were gamblers, carousers, drunkards; it was, in fact, the clergy that led the opposition to Wesley's spiritual movement.

But Wesley prevailed. How? By his famous preaching, certainly, and by that of the many godly men and women he rallied to his cause: "Give me one hundred preachers who fear nothing but sin and desire nothing but God ... such alone will shake the gates of hell." But even more than his preaching, even more than the dedication of his followers, it was *prayer* that enabled Wesley to overcome. He often said, "God does nothing but through prayer," and he believed it and staked his work upon it.

Think about that for a moment. "God does nothing but through prayer." How firmly do we believe that? How vigorously do we act upon it? How aggressively do we apply it to the many obstacles and difficulties that beset us, our families, our friends, our cities, our nations, our churches? How well do we avail ourselves of the vision, the wisdom, the power that waits for us in prayer?

We are spiritual beings, who live and move and have our being in the realm of spirit. Hence prayer is critical as the underpinning of our whole life, not just for its usefulness in "solving our problems." The key to living fully and freely in the kingdom of God is prayer.

We simply *must* learn to pray.

Lord, open our eyes to the spiritual realities that surround us. Impress upon our hearts the importance of prayer, apart from which we can do nothing. Teach us to pray, that we might better avail ourselves of your grace, your truth, and your power, and might more decisively bring your light and life into the circumstances of our lives.

For reflection and discussion:

—How clearly do I see the spiritual aspects of my daily reality?

—How can I learn to rely less on my own wisdom and effort and more on the power of God?

Part II

Teach Us to Pray

FIVE

Model Prayer

Lord, teach us to pray. (Lk 11:1)

THE GOSPELS MAKE IT EMINENTLY CLEAR that Jesus was a man of prayer. Before every major decision that faced him, before every significant turning point in his ministry, in the midst of every crisis that confronted him, we see him consulting with his Father in prayer. Time and again the gospel writers tell us of Jesus retreating to a lonely place and praying to his Father in heaven.

But evidently he did not do all his praying in secret. Evidently much of his prayer life was quite visible to his disciples. We would expect this, of course; in any master-disciple relationship, the master would have made it a high priority to set an example for his followers in something so foundational as prayer.

The disciples saw Jesus at prayer. And they were attracted by what they saw. So much so, in fact, that they were unwilling to settle simply for a good example; they went out of their way to ask Jesus to give them explicit instruction. "He was praying in a certain place," Luke recounts, "and when he ceased, one of his disciples said to him, 'Lord, teach us to pray, as John taught his disciples'" (Lk 11:1).

The disciples *wanted* to pray. One of the problems we often have with prayer is that we see it as an obligation, a duty. It *is* that, of course, but it is not *merely* that. When we see prayer solely as an obligation, as something we "have to do," we lose the joy of it. God helps us to move beyond seeing prayer as merely an obligation and enables us to see it as a privilege. When we pray, we want to see ourselves not as a starving man resignedly approaching a barren table in search of a few crumbs, but as coming to a feast, with great anticipation, to feed upon the living God himself. We want to come with the same eagerness the disciples showed when they asked Jesus to teach them how to pray.

Behind that request lay the disciples' experience of seeing Jesus as a man of prayer; a man whose life was marked by love, by power, by joy, which they must have associated with his time spent in intimate communion with God. They had seen him rise early in the morning to pray. They had seen him stay up late into the night to pray. And they had seen the fruit it had borne in his life. It is as if they said, "I want what I see in you. If prayer can do that for you, Lord, then teach me how to do it, too."

If we want to be like Jesus—if we want to experience love and joy and power and communion with God as Jesus did—then we too must learn how to pray as Jesus prayed.

Jesus answered the disciples' request by teaching them what we have come to call the Lord's Prayer. Thus the Lord's Prayer is both a prayer and a lesson about prayer. We can recite it as a prayer in its own right, and we can take it as a model for prayer more broadly. That, in fact, is a good way to think about it: as a model prayer given us by the model pray-er.

We can think about the Lord's prayer in three parts. The first part has to do with worship and adoration: *Our Father, who are in heaven, hallowed be thy name.* After that comes prayer for the furtherance of God's reign in the world: *Thy kingdom come, thy will be done, on earth as it is in heaven.* And only then, after we have first adored God and prayed for his work, do we pray for our own needs: *Give us this day . . .*

Our tendency, of course, is to reverse the order. We so often begin with our needs, our wants, our hurts, our desires. Sometimes that is not only where we begin, but also where we end: we become so absorbed in our own concerns that we never get around to praying for God's concerns, much less to worshiping and adoring him.

A few years ago I took my family on a trip to England. It was quite an expedition: myself, my wife, my three daughters, and my mother. Do you have any idea how much baggage it requires to get that many people overseas for a visit? We had to borrow several suitcases and trunks. And I didn't even try to bring along my guitar or my golf clubs!

The catch was this: we were making this trip only a few weeks after I had undergone minor surgery. I was well enough to travel, but I was not able to lift anything. So there I stood, baggage strewn all over the place, and me powerless to do anything with it. It was a very humbling experience to realize that I couldn't do anything for myself, but was completely dependent on my family and on the porters to move everything for me.

I believe most of us come into the presence of God with a lot of spiritual and emotional baggage. It's strewn all over the place. We need this, we need that, we hurt here, we hurt there, my marriage needs help, my job needs help, our children need help, I need a husband (or wife): we can't decide which piece of baggage to unload on the Lord first. Instead of praying, we spend our time thinking about our problems. We spend our time worrying instead of worshiping. We rise from our knees just as weary and frustrated as when we first knelt to pray.

If we are to pray as Jesus prayed, if we are to follow the model prayer given us by the model pray-er, we must learn to put first things first. We must recognize that we, too, are powerless to cope with the difficulties that surround us, that we are dependent on our Lord to handle them for us. There will be time enough later to bring to the Lord our seemingly endless list of needs and wants. First we must learn to worship him, and to see our needs in terms of his kingdom and his work upon the earth. That is how Jesus prayed. That is how we wish to pray. Let us begin.

Lord Jesus, we long to be like you, to experience life as you did in the fullness of grace and the Holy Spirit. We want to be men and women of prayer. Lord, as you taught your first disciples, teach us also to pray.

For reflection and discussion:

—Does my prayer get out of order, placing my own needs and decisions ahead of worship and adoration?

—What are some "pieces of baggage" I must learn to set aside when I approach God in prayer?

SIX

Intimacy and Adoration

Our Father, who art in heaven, hallowed be thy name.

THE LORD'S PRAYER BEGINS WITH INTIMACY. *Our Father.* We have become so used to reciting these words that we miss their impact. When Jesus taught his disciples to address God as their Father, it was a revelation. The Jews did not refer to God as Father in their general address to him.

The Christian, though, can use the word with the full force of its intimacy. The apostle Paul, in his letter to the Romans, says we may be so bold as to call him "Abba." In Hebrew, of course, "Abba" is the familiar word for father. It is the way sons and daughters addressed their father in the normal course of daily life. In our day, it is more or less equivalent to "Daddy." Although we may know some who have drifted into constant and exaggerated casualness with God, it is not too strong to say we are being positively encouraged to address him as "Daddy." That is well within the clear meaning of the term "Abba."

When we kneel in prayer, we should recognize that we kneel in the presence, not of a distant, remote God, but of a personal, intimate Father. He is a Father who cares for us, who wants to listen to us even more than we want to speak to him. He is a Father who wants good for us and not evil. *What man of you, if his son asks him for bread, will instead give him a stone? How much more will your Father who is in heaven give good things to those who ask him!* He is a Father who knows us inside and out. *Before him no creature is hidden, but all are open and laid bare to the eyes of him with whom we have to do.* He is a Father who cares for us personally and individually. *I am the good shepherd: I know my own and my own know me.*

But no sooner have we come into God's presence as before a loving Father than we also find ourselves face-to-face with the transcendent God, the mighty creator and awesome ruler of all that exists: Our Father *who art in heaven.* God encourages intimacy, but he does not simply call us into a casual buddy-buddy relationship. He draws near to us, but he also remains enthroned in glory. He is both immanent and transcendent; both intimate and intimidating.

Hallowed be thy name. In other words, "may your greatness be extolled and your name held in highest honor." This is a call to worship.

The book of Revelation paints a compelling word-picture of God seated on his throne, receiving worship and adoration from the myriads of heavenly creatures that surround him. "Day and night they never cease to sing, 'Holy, holy, holy, is the Lord God Almighty, who was and is and is to come'" (Rv 4:8). When we come to God in prayer, we come to adore him also. We come into the courts of heaven, and stand before his throne of majesty, and join the angels and archangels and all the company of heaven who laud and magnify the glory and majesty of God.

Worship is not something alien to our nature as human beings. It is part of what we were made for. Humans have a built-in longing to worship.

This is what lies behind our attraction to heroes, celebrities, sports stars, and the like. I have occasionally been invited to speak at chapel services for professional football teams when they are in town for their Sunday games. I am often struck by the crowds of people who gather in the hotel lobby, hoping to get a glimpse of the players. Sometimes, especially with the younger ones, I see in their faces the unmistakable glow of what can only be called a form of worship.

There is something in us that wants to look up to something greater than ourselves. The highest form of that "something" is to stand in awe of the majesty and grandeur of God. It is a built-in longing. We may be inexperienced or uneducated about how to give expression to it, but it is there. As we resolve to make worship the starting point of our prayer, it will begin to assert itself.

Moreover, we *need* to worship. It is vital to a healthy prayer life.

First of all, it puts our own problems in proper perspective. The world seems far more complicated when we dwell on circumstances rather than on God. Sometimes just reflecting on the greatness and majesty of God, rather than simply reciting our "shopping list" of needs and wants, solves half our problems without our even asking God for anything!

Second, our own personhood becomes better integrated when we dwell on God. We so often come to God scattered, fragmented. Being in his presence, acknowledging him, directing our gaze upon him, gives us a focal point around which our fractious lives can be drawn together in wholeness. It is said that man has, at the core of his being, a God-shaped vacuum, an emptiness only God can fill. We are like a jigsaw puzzle with a central piece missing. When we worship God we place him at the center of our being. We enable him to fill that emptiness that nothing else can fill, without which our life cannot be complete.

Third, worship is one of the things that makes us more God-like. "And we all, with unveiled face, beholding the glory of God, are being changed into his likeness from one degree of glory to another; for this comes from the Lord who is the spirit" (2 Cor 3:18). Something spiritual happens to us when we stand in God's presence and direct our gaze upon him in worship. As we behold the glory of God, we ourselves are raised from one degree of glory to another, by the work of the

Holy Spirit whose aim it is to make us more like God.

In Psalm 46, the Lord tells us, "Be still, and know that I am God. I am exalted among the nations, I am exalted in the earth!" (Ps 46:10). That is where our prayer must begin, in stillness, in recognition that we stand before a God who is a loving Father and yet Lord of all the earth. His name demands honor. His glory deserves exaltation. His majesty and grandeur evoke worship.

> *Almighty God, help us to recognize you as our Father. Father, help us to acknowledge you as the almighty God. Teach us to hallow your name and extol your greatness. Bring us into your heavenly courts that we may worship you. Help us to be still before you, and know your greatness, and exalt you amid the problems and concerns of our lives.*

For reflection and discussion:

—How fully do I recognize God as my loving Father?

—Do I devote an adequate portion of my prayer time to worship and adoration?

SEVEN

Under God's Reign

Thy kingdom come, thy will be done, on earth as it is in heaven.

AFTER ALIGNING OUR FOCUS by leading us to worship God our Father, the Lord's Prayer proceeds to bring us to the kingdom of God.

This seems quite natural. If the focus of our attention is God himself, if we have come into his courts and given ourselves over to adoration and praise, it is natural that his interests will become our interests, that we will want to pray for the things that concern him before we pray for those that concern us. When we are "into" the King we are "into" his kingdom.

Thy kingdom come. As soon as we begin to talk about the kingdom of God, there are three things we must recognize.

First, by the fact of acknowledging that there is a kingdom of God, we are also acknowledging that there is a kingdom of Satan. If there is a kingdom of light, then there is also a kingdom of darkness. There is no neutral territory, no unaligned spiritual realm over which there is no leadership—as if our task were merely to lead people out of neutrality and into God's camp. There are two kingdoms, one ruled by God and the other by Satan, and everything falls into one or the other.

This explains so much of what we see around us. We ask, Why is the world in such a mess? Why is it that industry, politics, even religion, seem always to be rushing headlong into misery? Why do husbands and wives seem to have such difficulties with each other? Why do children seem inevitably to rebel against tradition and authority? Why does everything always seem to go from bad to worse?

The reason is that there is a kingdom of evil at work in the world. Satan is a destroyer. He wants to destroy marriages. He wants to destroy families. He wants to destroy society and set nations at war one with another. He wants to see people nurture hatred in their hearts. The worse things get, the better he likes it. Satan hates you and has a terrible plan for your life!

So we recognize that there are two kingdoms, one bending every effort to destroy and overturn the other, and we pray that God's kingdom will overcome Satan's in us and in the world around us.

Second, when we speak of the kingdom of God, we must acknowledge that God really is the king, the ruler, the absolute sovereign. He has, as it were, a mind and will of his own. God is not running a democracy. When we pray for his kingdom, we are not casting a ballot in some sort of cosmic election.

"Thy will be done on earth *as it is in heaven.*" How thoroughly do you suppose God's will is done in heaven? Does he ever get an argument from those he rules? Are his viewpoints ever challenged? Are his commands ever disregarded? Obviously not. What he says goes. His slightest bidding is obeyed. His will is perfectly and completely realized. Not only that, but his will brings peace and joy to all concerned.

So, we pray, may it be on earth! When we pray for the coming of the kingdom, we are praying that God's mind, his view of things, must prevail over all others. We are praying that his will might be fully and completely realized in all human affairs. We are praying that all things might come under the sovereign reign of God who is king of the universe.

Third, when we speak of the kingdom of God we are not talking about territorial prerogatives. God's kingdom cannot be found on a map. God's kingdom means God's reign. When God rules in the hearts of men and women, *there* is the kingdom of God. It spans all nationalities. It cuts across all cultural barriers. It speaks all languages. It transcends all earthly power and authority. It is not subject to earthly political and economic systems. Wherever Jesus Christ is honored and obeyed as Lord, there is the kingdom of God.

Thus, when we pray for the coming of the kingdom of God, we are praying that God rule in the hearts of all men and women, that he be acknowledged as the king of all kings and the superior of all earthly authorities. We are praying, not that any group or class or nation or system be exalted, but that all be drawn together in God and under God, that God become all in all.

A friend of mine used to say he took his daily quiet time with his Bible in one hand and the morning paper in the other because he knew that secular affairs are also God's affairs. He didn't try to separate them as though they had nothing to do with each other. Because he knew the world of men had to come under the reign of God, he made that world a matter for prayer.

What does this mean for us? I can make several practical suggestions.

Pray for the affairs and problems of the world. When you scan the newspaper or watch the evening news on television, don't just write off international matters as remote and vexing problems over which you have no influence. Pray about them.

In that context, pray for missionaries, for those who struggle to bring the reign of God into the hearts of men and women in remote parts of the world. Most of us cannot become missionaries ourselves, but we can take part in the missionary work of the church through prayer.

Pray for national affairs. Do you know that with God there is no separation of church and state? He is not sitting up there in heaven, scratching his head and saying, "My, my, my. How am I going to get around this problem? I'm restricted to working within the church." In God's mind, there is absolutely no problem with trying to spiritually redirect the course of secular events, even of government and politics. The secular world will never isolate God on a "religious reservation."

In the same way, we can pray for our state, our county, our city. We can pray for our businesses and industries, our schools, our leaders. We can pray—had better pray—for our churches.

Last of all, we can pray for ourselves—that the kingdom of God come in our own lives, that God reign over our hearts and minds, that his will be done there just as it is in heaven. Pray that God's kingdom come in your job, your office, your relationships, your neighborhood, your marriage, your family, your trade union, your athletic club—the list is endless. It is as we pray in this fashion that God prepares our hearts to pray properly for our personal needs, because he sees them in a larger perspective that we can, and because his answer can only come in the context of his kingdom, not in the context of our passing whims and feelings.

Lord, give us the courage to pray for the coming of your kingdom. We know that many things will have to change, in us and in others. Whatever it takes, give us the courage to pray for it and the means to bring it about. May your will be done in us, and on the whole earth as it is in heaven.

For reflection and discussion:

—How thoroughly do I grasp God's absolute sovereignty over the world and all that fills it including my own life?

—Are there any particular areas where God has given me a special burden to pray for the coming of his kingdom?

EIGHT

The Great Secret

Give us this day our daily bread.

IT IS, IN A WAY, SURPRISING that we find so mundane a request as "give us our daily bread" right at the heart of the Lord's Prayer. Yet this tells us something of the importance the Lord places on our simple, basic needs.

We sometimes feel embarrassed bringing our personal needs and problems to the Lord. Here we are, in the courts of the God of all the universe, talking about these picayune details of life that weigh so heavily upon us. After all, what difference does it make to God and to his plan for the cosmos whether our car gets fixed on time, or whether we get some extra money, or even whether we avoid missing a meal here and there?

But apparently our needs *do* make a difference to him. He himself has taught us to pray for them. Having placed our prayer in the context of communication with a loving Father, then of the adoration of the King of creation, then of longing for the full flowering of God's reign over all earthly affairs, Jesus brings us, in his model prayer, to our own personal needs. *Give us this day our daily bread.*

We cannot, in fact, learn to pray properly for our needs apart for this larger context. That is one of the lessons of the Lord's Prayer. It is only after we pray in terms of God's fatherhood and in terms of his kingdom that we pray for ourselves. The Lord Jesus, by his example, teaches us to come to him, not need-centered or self-centered, but God-centered and kingdom-centered. Our prayer is not to be in the spirit of "give me, give me, give me," but in the light of the grander purpose of God for his world and our lives.

When we are self-centered in our prayer we twist the meaning of God's promises to provide for us, and we distort our relationship with him. We are not the center of the universe! He is!

We all know that Jesus makes some breathtaking statements about God's care for us and his eagerness to provide for us. "If two of you agree on earth about anything they ask, it will be done for them by my Father in heaven" (Mt 18:19). "Truly, truly, I say to you, if you ask anything of the Father, he will give it to you in my name" (Jn 16:23). When we are need-centered in our prayer we hold God to these promises in an ugly, selfish way. "Okay, God, the two of us agree on this. Now give it to us!"

I often hear people pray this way, and it grieves me. Who, after all, is Lord and who the servant? When we pray like this, it is as though we were putting ourselves in charge and making God answerable to us, holding him hostage to our selfish interpretation of his promise.

A similar problem sometimes arises with the phrase, "in the name of Jesus." This phrase is sometimes used almost as if it were a kind of magical incantation: we pray as we like, then tack on the phrase, "in Jesus' name," and thus obligate God to do what we say!

But to pray "in the name of Jesus" means more than just to sprinkle our prayers with the word "Jesus." It means to pray *according to the character of Jesus.*

The use of names in scripture has more to do with character and content than we are used to in the West. It speaks of identity, not merely of identification. A person's name is not just a label but a representation of that person's character.

When God sovereignly intervenes in someone's life and changes his or her character, he signifies it by giving a new name. Thus Abram became Abraham, Sarai became Sarah, Simon became Peter, Saul became Paul. To pray in Jesus' name means to pray according to his mind, for his purposes, in line with his character, on behalf of his dignity.

The character of Jesus was to do the will of his Father in heaven. He put his Father's purposes ahead of his own. "For I have come down from heaven, not to do my own will, but the will of him who sent me" (Jn 6:38). "Father, if thou art willing, remove this cup from me; nevertheless not my will, but thine, be done" (Lk 22:42).

It must be the same with us. We must place God's will ahead of our own. When we do this, our prayer for our needs changes in an important way. No longer are we selfishly demanding that God serve our whims. Rather, we claim his promises as his servants, so that we can advance his cause and further his plan.

This is the great secret: God meets our needs, not so that things will go *our* way but so they can go *his* way; not so that we can have our way, but so that he can have his. God actually glorifies himself and brings about his kingdom through caring for his people and meeting their needs. When we approach him in that spirit we see the fulfillment of his promises in their proper light.

The fact is that everything in our lives, even those things that seem the most mundane and trivial, have significance in God's will for our lives. When God shows concern for the seemingly inconsequential details in our lives, it does not represent an excursion from his plan, but an expression of it. If may be—in fact, it usually is—hard for us to *see* the significance. But that is of little importance. What *is* important is that God sees their significance, and that when we bring them to him as his children, in the context of his kingdom, he is able to work with them and through them for the advancement of his fatherly vision. Thus, praying for our daily concerns is not merely a privilege God grants us—a special concession to our weakness and need—but a vital part of his plan. When we bring the details of our daily life to the Lord in prayer, we give him the opportunity to mold and direct them, and to work his will through them.

> *Father in heaven, you know our every need even before we ask. You know how every detail of our lives can be fitted into your plan for our life and your plan for the whole world. We bring our needs to you, trusting in you to care for us as your children and work through us as your servants.*

For reflection and discussion:

—Is my prayer marked by selfishness in demanding that God answer my request according to my timetable and preferences?

—How can I learn to pray for my own needs as God's servant and according to the character of Jesus?

NINE

The Miracle Cure

Forgive us our debts, as we also forgive our debtors.

THERE ARE MANY SPIRITUAL SICKNESSES that poison our lives with the Lord. We suffer from bitterness: from the aching anger that cries out for revenge against another, whether it be a "big" revenge ("I could kill that person") or a little one ("The next time I see him I'm going to tell him just what I think of him"). We suffer from self-pity: from hanging on the four walls of our consciousness full-color portraits of all the wrongs, real and perceived, that others have done to us. We suffer from feelings of failure and guilt: over a marriage that failed, a child gone wrong, a job botched and lost. We suffer from despair and frustration over broken relationships: relationships we so badly want to have right but see no way of making right.

Jesus offers a cure for all these sicknesses and many more besides: forgiveness.

Forgive us our debts, as we also forgive our debtors. In this line from the Lord's Prayer, Jesus actually talks about two kinds of forgiveness: God's forgiveness of us, and our forgiveness of one another. Clearly the two are related to one another.

But they are not related to one another in quite the way we so often think. We sometimes interpret this teaching as a kind of cosmic tit-for-tat. "You forgive others," we imagine God saying, "*then* I'll forgive you. Otherwise, no dice."

Surely we know God better than that! As Donald Coggan, the former archbishop of Canterbury, put it in his book *The Prayers of the New Testament*: "To think of this as a kind of *quid pro quo* prayer—if we forgive those who wrong us, then forgiveness is our due—is, of course, completely to misunderstand it. Rather, we have in this clause a principle laid down, a hard fact stated: if we refuse to forgive, then we so harden ourselves that the forgiveness of God cannot reach us. We grow an impenetrable callous of the soul. We hurt ourselves far more than we hurt other people."

If we are unwilling to forgive, it is not that God refuses to forgive us, but that we make ourselves unforgivable. The obstacle is in us, not in God. God's forgiveness is still there for us, but it cannot reach us because our soul is calloused, our heart hardened.

Who is it that you are unwilling to forgive? If I were to gather almost any group of people—even devout Christians—into a room and ask all those to stand who have in their minds some individual they absolutely do not wish to forgive, I suspect almost everyone would stand up.

Who is it that *you* are unwilling to forgive? Someone who took advantage of you, hurt you deeply, long ago—or maybe not so long ago? A parent? A child? A spouse? A business associate? A teacher?

Many years ago, when I was working as youth minister in a church, there was one particular teenager who so antagonized me that he made my life and ministry miserable. I disliked him so strongly I could hardly make myself go to the boys' club that I ran three nights a week. He sneered at me. He used offensive language and exhibited a belligerent attitude. He took every opportunity to belittle me. I can still remember his name clearly. (That I can still remember the name of the one boy I dislike, and have forgotten the names of so many who were a joy to be with, is in itself a testimonial to the power of my bitterness.)

We used to play an indoor version of soccer, and I could hardly wait to get out onto the court with him on the opposite team. When he came into view I was no longer interested in the ball; I was interested only in him. What really riled me was that he so obviously felt the same way about me. We would drive each other against the walls and into the pillars that supported the roof. All this in a Christian boys' club! And me an ordained Christian minister!

Obviously this couldn't go on. I simply had to overcome my nauseating ill will toward this young man.

One afternoon I got down on my knees and brought myself and him to Jesus. In my prayer I said, "Lord, I see him kneeling before your cross. I see you looking down on him, loving him, dying for him. You love him as much as you love me. You died for him in the same way you died for me. Help me to love him the way you do. Help me to see him through your eyes." It wasn't easy, but *I was determined not to give up praying until "my heart" was changed.* I remember saying, "Lord, I'm not getting up off my knees until I see him as you see him, and love him as you love him." And, praise God, he did it.

In our small, narrow, human arena, forgiveness may seem impossible. But in God's arena, at the cross of Christ, it *is* possible. If you try to deal with it within yourself—if your only frame of reference is the pain you've absorbed and the anger on which you've fed yourself—you're in deep trouble. But if you deal with it at the cross, God begins to deal with you and makes you new by his love and mercy. God's will for the other person's life is that they receive forgiveness both from him and from you. The cross is where that happens.

Who *is* it that you are unwilling to forgive? There is only one way to do it. You must bring them before the cross of Jesus. Recognize that you have no more merit before Jesus than they do, that in the eyes of the pure and righteous one you are no more deserving of God's love than they are. How can you kneel before God and say, "Forgive me for hating him," without also saying, "Lord, forgive him, love him, and help me to love and forgive him as you do."

Now we can talk about God's forgiveness of you. As the Lord softens your heart so you become open to experiencing his forgiveness.

And God *wants* you to experience it! The Greek word that we translate "forgive" means to let go, to turn loose, to release. God can release us! He can release us from the bitterness, from the anger, the self-pity, the frustration and despair that flow from unforgiveness.

The fact, of course, is that God has already forgiven us in Christ, if we belong to Christ. It is not so much a question of winning a forgiveness we do not have as of experiencing the forgiveness that is already ours in Christ. It is there for us; we have only to reach out and grasp it.

The story is told—a true story, by the way—of a group of men who had been shipwrecked and were adrift in the Atlantic Ocean in a small lifeboat. The drinking water they had brought with them was gone, and they were dying of thirst. They knew that if they drank the sea water that surrounded them, the salt would only increase their thirst and drive them to madness.

After days of agonizing thirst, a large ship appeared on the horizon, spotted them and came to their rescue. The stranded men cried out, through parched lips, "Give us something to drink! Lower some water to us!" One of the sailors on the rescue ship called back, "Take some of the water around you and drink!" The shipwrecked men thought they were being mocked.

But the truth of the matter was this. Though they were indeed adrift in the Atlantic Ocean, they were not in salt water but in fresh. They were out of sight of land, but were in fact in the mouth of the Amazon River, which is so mighty a river that where it empties into the ocean, it pushes fresh water hundreds of miles out into the sea.

How many of us are like them? We have come to the cross and claimed the forgiveness of Christ, but we have not drunk of it. It is all around us and we do not realize it, do not seize upon it. Forgiveness is a fact, but it is not part of our experience. First we must open ourselves to receive it by granting forgiveness to others. This all takes place at the foot of the cross. We must simply "take and drink."

> *Lord, forgive us for our very unforgiveness. Transform our lives with your forgiveness so that we may see and love others as you do. Then open our eyes to the grace and mercy that surrounds us so that we drink deeply of your forgiveness.*

For reflection and discussion:

—Are there any people against whom I am harboring bitterness and unforgiveness?

—How can I learn to take hold of the forgiveness God has provided for me in his Son Jesus?

TEN

Trial and Error

Lead us not into temptation, but deliver us from evil.

LET US STEP BACK FOR A MOMENT and look at the Lord's Prayer as a whole. We begin, as we have seen, acknowledging God as our Father and as our Lord: *Our Father, who art in heaven, hallowed be thy name.* We then move to praying for God's concerns: *Thy kingdom come, thy will be done, on earth as it is in heaven.*

Then we pray for ourselves, in the form of three petitions. Two of these petitions we have already considered, the third we shall consider in this chapter. But what I want us to see is how the doctrine of the Trinity is inherent in the Lord's Prayer as we bring our personal needs to God.

When we pray, *Give us this day our daily bread,* we acknowledge God the Father, who loves us, cares for us, providing for our needs. When we pray, *Forgive us our debts,* we acknowledge God the Son, who died on the cross for our salvation, forgives us, enables us to forgive others. Now as we pray, *Lead us not into temptation,* we acknowledge God the Holy Spirit, who leads us, protects us, empowers us and works God's purposes in us.

Let's be honest. We struggle with the implications of this prayer. It seems clear that Jesus is telling us to ask God not to lead us to sin. But to pray this way is to open the door to the proposition that *unless* we pray, God actually *might* lead us to sin. Is that possible? Would God really lead us to sin? The petition begins to sound like a prayer of defense against God. Unless we specifically beg him not to, might he lead us astray? Surely God would not be so cruel!

Indeed he would not. The truth of the matter is this. God *does* lead us into times of trial and temptation, but he does *not* lead us into sin.

Jesus himself provides the clearest example of this. After being baptized by John in the Jordan, Jesus "was led up by the Spirit into the wilderness *to be tempted by the devil*" (Mt 4:1). It was God the Holy Spirit who led him into a time of the most intense spiritual warfare. This buffeting was not outside God's plan for his Son, but was part of the preparation of the Lord Jesus for his ministry. In fact it was this time of temptation that gave clarity to his mission. God led him into a time of testing, but not into sin.

James makes the same point more straightforwardly. "Let no one say when he is tempted, 'I am tempted by God;' for God cannot be tempted with evil and he himself tempts no one, but each person is tempted when he is lured and enticed by his own desire" (Jas 1:13-14). In other words, God allows us to face temptation—sometimes he arranges things precisely so that we *will* face testing—but he himself does not do the tempting. Satan does, as in the case of Jesus; or, in our own case, desire does, as James explains; but God himself does not.

But why does God even open the door to times of testing? Why does he allow the devil, or our desires, to tempt us? Would we not be better off without it?

No doubt our heart's desire is to be spared all trial and difficulty. But if God were to answer that prayer according to our desire, we would never be anything but weak, flabby Christians.

The reason God allows—even arranges—times of testing for us is that these experiences strengthen us. "Count it all joy, my brethren, when you meet various trials," James says, "for you know that the testing of your faith produces steadfastness. And let steadfastness have its full effect, that you may be perfect and complete, lacking in nothing" (Jas 1:2-4). Steadfast Christians are not produced in a soft climate of easy acceptance, but in the crucible of testing. That is why we embrace trials: not because they are good or enjoyable in themselves, but because they make us stronger.

And yet the prayer does say, "Lead us *not* into temptation." How are we to reconcile this with what we have seen about the importance of embracing testing?

This petition is expression of the human heart. Jesus himself shared in it. As he knelt in the Garden of Gethsemane, knowing what trials lay ahead for him, he prayed with a fervor so strong that he sweated, as it were, great drops of blood, "Father, if thou art willing, remove this cup from me; nevertheless not my will, but thine, be done" (Lk 22:42).

This is the same Jesus who gives us our model prayer, who understands our humanness and teaches us to cry out in that humanness even as he did, but who knows that God's will for us may yet be to bring us into a time of testing, even as God's will for him was that the cup of suffering not be taken away.

As with Jesus in the wilderness, God never allows us to undergo a test we cannot handle if only we will rely on him. "God is faithful, and he will not let you be tempted beyond your strength, but with the temptation will also provide the way of escape, that you may be able to endure it" (1 Cor 10:13).

What is most important is that we learn to see these times of testing from God's perspective. We are looking for ease and comfort; God is looking for Christlikeness. Any testing God allows us to undergo is for our strengthening.

Joni Eareckson is a young woman who was paralyzed from the neck down in a tragic accident nearly twenty years ago. She lives in a wheelchair. For most of us that would be an overwhelming trial. But God has given her the ability to endure it, and has used it to make her a great Christian. Here is how she describes her life on her album *Spirit Wings* where she sings so beautifully:

Though I spend my mortal lifetime in this chair
I refuse to waste it living in despair
And though others may receive
Gifts of healing, I believe
that he has given me a gift beyond compare.

For heaven is nearer to me
And at times it is all I can see
Sweet music I hear
coming down to my ear
And I know that it's playing for me.

For I am Christ the Savior's own bride
And redeemed I shall stand by his side
He will say, Shall we dance?
And our endless romance
Will be worth all the tears I have cried.

Lord, we do pray in our humanness and frailty that you would not lead us into temptation. But even as we do, we thank you for the times of testing you have brought our way. Help us to see them from your point of view, and to embrace them so that they may be times of blessing and strengthening.

For reflection and discussion:

—Are there any areas where I am resisting God's desire to strengthen me through testing?

—How can I learn to rely on God's strength in overcoming temptations that come my way?

ELEVEN

The Devil: His Style Is Wile

Deliver us from evil.

I HATE TO GIVE any "air time" to the devil. I would rather not speak of him at all. But Jesus includes a reference to him in his model prayer—this line can just as correctly be translated "deliver us from *the evil one*"—because he knows how important it is that we know our enemy and how to deal with him.

Nowadays we try to explain away belief in Satan. We tell ourselves he's just a psychological device; we recognize within ourselves a tendency toward evil that we don't understand and can't control, so we create "the devil" as a scapegoat for our own shortcomings.

Even if this rationalization worked in terms of you and me, it doesn't explain Jesus. Jesus makes clear all through the gospels that he believes in Satan's existence. And as the incarnate Son of God, Jesus had no propensity toward evil that needed to be explained away by a psychological device. If we are to believe the scriptures, we must believe in the existence of the one scripture calls the devil, or Satan, or Lucifer.

C.S. Lewis noted that one of the devil's great triumphs is to persuade us that he does not exist. If we refuse to acknowledge his existence, we certainly won't take any steps to defend ourselves against him. And then we're sitting ducks. We must first settle it in our minds that the devil is a real, live person with whom we must deal.

The next thing we need to recognize about Satan is that he is a destroyer. "Be sober, be watchful," Peter warns us. "Your adversary the devil prowls around like a roaring lion, seeking some one to devour" (1 Pt 5:8).

What does Satan seek to destroy? You; your marriage; if you're single, your chastity; your relationships: parent to child, husband to wife, friend to friend, employer to employee. He especially wants to destroy your relationship to God. He wants to destroy your mind, your emotions, your character. He wants to destroy your church, your city, your nation. Anything that is good in your life, Satan wants to destroy. He is like a ravenous lion, starved for chaos and ruin, seeking out anything to destroy. So we must ever be on guard against him.

The next time you're about to say something that tears down a fellow believer, remember who's standing at your shoulder, urging, "Go ahead, say it." When you're rushing headlong into self-pity, telling yourself, "I'm no good. Nobody loves me," remember who's whispering in your ear, saying, "Go ahead, believe it." When you're feeding your anger at a friend or associate, thinking of ways to "get back," remember who's nudging you, saying, "Go ahead, do it." Don't listen to that crafty, lying voice.

Next, the devil's style is wile. He operates by deception. Remember his words to Eve in the Garden? Lies from beginning to end! What is he really saying? *I love you, Eve. I'm on your side.* That's a lie. *I want what's best for you.* That's another lie. *Actually, I'm more concerned for your welfare than God is.* A monstrous lie. *Go ahead. Eat the fruit. You'll have a better life. Why, you'll be just like God!* The cruelest lie of all.

Satan was even bold enough to lie to Jesus. *Take care of yourself first, Jesus; turn these stones into bread. Put on a good show for us; throw yourself off the temple and call out the angels to save you from death. Don't put yourself through the agony of the cross;*

worship me and I'll give you all the kingdoms of the world. It was all
a lie and deception. Jesus knew enough to resist Satan's lies. So
must we.

Next, his target is the Christian. "He goes around seeking. . . ." One Sunday I mentioned to my associate pastor that I
was going to preach about the devil. "He'll be there to hear it,"
he reminded me. If Satan didn't shy away from attacking Jesus,
he certainly won't hesitate to attack his church. He doesn't
have to work that hard in drug-saturated rock concerts or
pornographic shows; he's got those locked up. The place he's
working overtime in is the church of Jesus Christ. He wants to
destroy our prayer, our preaching, our fellowship. He wants to
destroy our evangelism and outreach.

But the good news is that in Jesus Christ, Satan has been
defeated and his work cast down. "The reason the Son of God
appeared was to destroy the works of the devil" (1 Jn 3:8).
Through the cross of Christ and its power at work in our lives,
we can be "more than conquerors" over the wiles of Satan.

Our part, Peter says, is to "resist him" (1 Pt 5:9). The
Reverend Terry Fullam, rector of St. Paul's Episcopal Church
in Darien, Connecticut, describes it this way. The devil, he
says, is firmly chained, but there is a certain area within his
reach. Outside that area he cannot touch you. It is within that
area that he roars and roams and seeks to devour. If you step
within his reach, you've put yourself in danger. Satan's
deception is in making the chain appear shorter than it is. He
tries to lull us into thinking we can come closer to spiritual
danger than we know is safe. That is how he tempts us. *Come
closer. It'll be all right. Take another step. There's nothing to worry
about. Come on in.*

In the power of Jesus, we can turn those temptations into
victories. Jesus turned the devil's lies against him and came
away the stronger for it. So with us; times of testing are meant
to lead us, not to step into the devil's territory, but to rely on
Jesus and put the devil to rout.

Lord Jesus, convince us of the reality and power of our enemy. But at the same time, convince us of the reality and power of your victory on the cross. Strengthen us against the wiles of the devil, and teach us to overcome his work by calling upon you.

For reflection and discussion:

—Do I acknowledge the reality of Satan and his work in the world and in my life?

—Are there parts of my life that Satan seems to be trying to destroy? Where do I need to resist and overcome him?

—Are there areas of my life where I put myself in danger by wandering too close to evil?

TWELVE

Glory, Glory, Hallelujah!

*Thine is the kingdom, and the power, and the glory,
now and forever.*

THE LORD'S PRAYER ENDS, as it began, with worship. We have come full circle. The heart of all prayer must be this adoration of God. It is the context in which we make our many other prayers, for our needs, for forgiveness, for strength to overcome temptation and endure testing. It is as we place ourselves in God's presence, there to love him and adore him, that those other prayers find their rightful focus. Whether we are asking for needs to be met or sins to be forgiven, it is all an act of worship.

Thine is the kingdom. Throughout all scripture, one fundamental truth is triumphantly, resoundingly reaffirmed over and over again. "Hallelujah! For the Lord our God the Almighty reigns" (Rv 19:6). God is on the throne. He is in charge. He is Lord of lords and King of kings. No matter what chaos appears around us, no matter what trials of men and nations, no matter what personal misfortunes, the Lord is King.

The Lord reigns; he is robed in majesty;
the Lord is robed, he is girded with strength.

> Yea, the world is established; it shall never be moved;
> thy throne is established from of old;
> thou art from everlasting. (Ps 93:1-2)

Reflect for a moment on the events leading up to Jesus' crucifixion. Has there ever been a more diabolical set of circumstances, a more insipid cast of characters, a more sordid course of events? And yet, amid all the betrayal and misery and cowardice, the sovereign Lord is working out his own purpose. He is Lord even over his own death. Nothing can frustrate his plan. That is the nature and degree of his kingly power and authority.

The same thing happens in our own lives. God reigns even over our difficulties. You have no doubt heard the expression, "When life gives you lemons, make lemonade." It is because of God's reign in our life that we can conceive of such a thing. Events and circumstances that could create tremendous bitterness become sources of blessing as we bring them to the Lord and invite him to use them for his purposes. What is bitter can make us better. The reign of God does not mean that everything is peaches and cream, but that lemons can be turned into lemonade.

Thine is the power. All power comes from God and belongs to God. Any power that we exercise, any gift or ability or skill, originates in God and finds its meaning in God.

Our tendency, of course, is to take the credit for ourselves when things go well, to attribute our blessings and successes to our own virtue and hard work. It is a universal phenomenon. Athletes take the credit for their physical prowess. Movie stars and models take the credit for their physical beauty. Students and teachers take the credit for their intellectual acumen.

God help us to see the truth! "What have you that you did not receive? If then you received it, why do you boast as if it were not a gift?" (1 Cor 4:7). "For all things come from thee, and of thy own have we given thee" (1 Chr 29:14).

Thine is the glory. "We who first hoped in Christ have been destined and appointed to live for the praise of his glory" (Eph 1:12). This will be the measure of our lives: for whom have we lived?

I once read a newspaper article about marriage that said, "the most important thing a father can do for his children is to love his wife, and the most important thing a mother can do for her children is to love her husband." There is sound wisdom in that. But the most important thing any of us can do is to live to the glory of God. Our lives aren't just for our husbands, or for our wives, or for our children, or even for ourselves, but for God. There is a profound impact made on all who live around us when we live with God as the ultimate focus. Give yourself to any other god and it will destroy you and those close to you. Give yourself to the Lord of glory, and that glory will shine and enhance all who come within your influence.

The other night I took our family dog for a walk. It was a full moon, so bright that we cast a shadow as we walked along. But of course the moon has no light of its own. It shone, and it lit us up so brightly, because the sun was shining on it. It merely reflected the sun's light.

In the same way, we have no glory of our own, only such as is reflected from the light of Christ that shines upon us. That is what we live for: to bask in that radiance, to reflect it, to bring it to the world around us, not for our own sake but for the praise of his glory.

As we conclude our reflections on the Lord's Prayer, the prayer our Lord taught us so that we might know *how* to pray, take it and make it your own. Pray your way through it and give every thought expressed by the Lord Jesus its full weight and measure. Don't use it as a talisman or something to be merely recited. Use it as the foundational expression of your worship of the Living God.

Our Father, who art in heaven, hallowed be thy name.
Thy kingdom come, thy will be done, on earth as it is in heaven.

Give us this day our daily bread, and forgive us our debts as we forgive our debtors.
And lead us not into temptation, but deliver us from evil.
For thine is the kingdom, and the power, and the glory, forever and forever.
   Amen.

For reflection and discussion:

—Do I approach difficulties in my life with confidence, knowing that Jesus is Lord of all?

—Do I acknowledge God as the source of my talents and abilities and use them so as to magnify his glory rather than my own?

Part III

Principles of Prayer

THIRTEEN

An Intimate Relationship

God has sent the Spirit of his Son into our hearts,
crying, "Abba! Father!" (Gal 4:6)

PRAYER IS FIRST AND FOREMOST an expression of an intimate relationship with God.

Prayer includes discipline, but it is not merely a discipline. It involves setting aside a regular time and place, but it is not merely an item on our schedule. It includes asking for things we need, but it is not merely a shopping list of requests and rejoicings. It involves us speaking to God and God speaking to us, but it is not merely an exchange of memoranda.

More than anything else, prayer is a *relationship*. When we reduce it to a regimen, we deprive ourselves of what all who knew God throughout the scriptures expressed in their prayers: that God is alive, that he knows us and lets himself be known by us, that we can enjoy a deep and intimate personal relationship with him in prayer.

But when the time had fully come, God sent forth his Son, born of woman, born under the law, to redeem those who were under the law, so that we might receive adoption as sons. And because you are sons, God has sent the Spirit of his Son into our hearts, crying, "Abba! Father!" So through God you are no longer a slave but a son, and if a son then an heir. (Gal 4:4-7)

We have already seen that *abba* was the Jewish equivalent of "daddy." When I come home in the evening, my little daughter Sarah comes toddling in to greet me, smiling and gurgling "daddy, daddy, daddy." To her, that is an expression not so much of the precise nature of our relationship (she is not yet old enough to comprehend that) but of intimacy with me. She does not yet understand that I am her father but she fully understands that I am her "daddy."

It is the same between God and us. We cannot fully comprehend the mysteries of the Godhead, but we can still know that God is our *Abba*. We can bask in the intimacy we enjoy with him.

We enjoy this intimacy, Paul teaches us, because we have been adopted into the family of God through the redeeming work of Jesus. We have not received a spirit of slavery, Paul emphasizes (Rom 8:14-15), but a spirit of sonship, of intimacy. When we are born of the Spirit and the Spirit comes to dwell within us, we are adopted as spiritual children into God's family.

People sometimes speak of all mankind as "the children of God." This is true only in a very limited sense. The limited sense in which God is the author of all creation, and humankind was originally created in his image. In that sense there is still the vestige of the "family resemblance." But in the full sense of which we are speaking, it is only those who have received Christ into their lives, whom the Holy Spirit has regenerated, who can know the intimacy that comes with *sonship*.

I once knew a distant, impersonal relationship with God. I had been brought up "Christian" in the usual vague, cultural way, and from time to time—especially when I was in difficult circumstances or in great need—I would try to pray to God. It was like shouting at the heavens or, as someone has said, like "talking to a brass sky." I would "talk at" God about my examinations at school, or my need for a job, or whatever. There was no sense whatever of "getting through" to anyone at the other end. I had no knowledge of God as someone close who knew me and cared about me.

All that was transformed the night I asked Christ into my life. I remember waking up the very next morning and thinking to myself, "I am not alone." I was eighteen years old at the time, in that developing of life (adolescence) where loneliness and alienation are felt so keenly. I walked out of the house and down the street that morning *knowing* that God walked with me, that I was not, and never would be, alone again.

The obvious, natural expression of this closeness to God is to talk to him. I would go so far as to encourage you, whenever it is feasible, to talk out loud to him. Certainly we can communicate with God mentally; our thoughts can readily be cast in words and sentences addressed to the Lord. But the intimacy of our relationship is enhanced when we speak to him out loud, when we *hear* ourselves speak to him.

Wives know it is not enough for their husbands simply to *think*, "Honey, I love you." Their husbands may indeed love them deeply and sincerely, and they may think about it fervently and often, but *thinking* it isn't enough. They need to *say* it.

Of course, God can "hear" our thoughts as well as our spoken words, so it is not primarily for his sake that we put them into words. It is for *our* sake. When a husband says to his wife, "Honey, I love you," it not only pleases her, it confirms it in him. So it is with prayer. It does something good for our spirit to actually *hear* ourselves pray. It helps draw us into an experience of the intimacy we enjoy with God in a way that purely mental prayer does not.

Further, speaking to God out loud helps us to maintain concentration and not to wander all over the place in our mind.

Father in heaven, help us to understand the intimacy we enjoy with you as your adopted children. Help us to come to know you as Abba. *Give us the freedom to speak to you as a child to a loving father, basking in the warmth of your love for us.*

For reflection and discussion:

—How fully do I experience the intimacy with God that comes from knowing I am his child?

—Do I practice praying aloud as a way of expressing my relationship with the Lord?

FOURTEEN

An Encompassing Relationship

In him we live and move and have our being. (Acts 17:28)

PRAYER, WE HAVE SAID, is an intimate relationship with a God who loves us and cares for us. Because of that, we can talk personally with him, one to one, as we would with another person. It is also important for us to understand that we can be completely open with God, can talk with him about anything and everything that is on our hearts.

Our relationship with God is all encompassing. It is not as though there were some segments of our life that were part of our relationship with God, and others that were segregated or set apart.

When God adopts us into his family, he adopts us in the totality of who we are. He doesn't love just parts of us, he loves all of us. He isn't concerned only about some aspects of our life, but about all aspects. There is no part of our lives, however insignificant it might seem to us, with which God is not intimately familiar and about which he does not care deeply. Everything in our lives happens in the presence of God, under the watchful eye of God, within the love and mercy of God. As Paul explained to the men of Athens, it is God in whom "we live and move and have our being" (Acts 17:28).

Because of this, there is no limitation to what we can or

should talk to God about in prayer. Now you often hear people speak as if there were parts of their life God did not take an interest in, parts that were too insignificant to bring before him. Or you hear people speak as if there were parts of their lives they were embarrassed to mention to God, as though he might think them foolish for being so concerned about them.

By thinking this way, we cheat ourselves out of what God wants us to experience in our relationship with him. We can be totally open in our relationship with God. He wants us to share all of our life with him. What concerns us concerns God, simply because he loves us. We can tell God our heart's longings. We can talk to him about the things that irritate us. We can speak frankly to him about people who are wounding us. We can ask his advice on matters that worry us. Everything in our life becomes part of our relationship with God.

The most dramatic instance of this in my own life, when I first became a Christian, was in terms of my relationship with girls. It was a revelation to me that God was interested in my dating life, not as a cold rule-enforcer trying to keep me from sinning (and, of course, from having fun), but as a Father genuinely concerned that I find his will in a very important part of my life. I didn't get married until I was thirty-one, and in many ways it was difficult to wait that long. But because I approached it in prayer I trusted that God was in charge and this protected me from rushing into marriage with the wrong woman. Now, of course, when I reflect on the wife God gave me, on our marriage and family and the countless blessings that have come through them, I see how intimately concerned God was with this part of my life and I am deeply grateful to him for welcoming me and watching over me—in love.

Even the seemingly trivial parts of our lives are included in our all encompassing relationship with God. When I was a teenager I was positively addicted to soccer. As I walked to school I would kick anything that moved, pretending it was a soccer ball. When I walked past a low-hanging tree branch I would leap up and "head it." In my mind I was kicking a soccer ball or delivering a perfect "header," right onto the foot of the forward who would slam it into the back of the goal net. I ate and drank and breathed and slept soccer.

When I became a Christian I didn't give up playing soccer, nor did I leave God out of my sporting life. I took God, as it were, onto the field with me. I would pray that I might honor him by the way I played that day. It just seemed natural to me. It wasn't that I heard a sermon one Sunday on how to serve the Lord through soccer. It was just that I experienced God as Lord of my whole life, concerned about every aspect of my life. So I brought even that seemingly trivial aspect of my life and gave it over to him.

It is amazing, the ways we persuade ourselves that God's love does not extend to this or that facet of our lives. Some things seem too small and insignificant; we don't want to "trouble" God. Some things seem too mundane; we don't want to "waste God's time" with them. Some things seem so embarrassing we are too shy to talk about them with God, as if he didn't already know all about them. Some things are so important to us we are almost reluctant to pray about them for fear God *won't* hear us; we're afraid of being "let down."

God helps us to see how unnecessary, how foolish, such fears and apprehensions are. There is nothing too small for him, nothing too mundane; nothing we need hold back for fear of losing his love, nothing we need fear in opening all our lives to him; nothing that could ever fall outside the bounds of his all-encompassing love for us, his children.

Lord, help us to realize that nothing in our life is insignificant to you, nothing is outside the bounds of your love and concern. Help us to understand the all-involving nature of your relationship to us so that we will not hesitate to bring every part of our life before you in prayer.

For reflection and discussion:

—Do I feel free to speak to God about every aspect of my life?

—Are there areas I am "holding back" from God because I fail to appreciate his all-encompassing love for me?

FIFTEEN

A Constant Relationship

Pray without ceasing. (1 Thes 5:17)

OUR RELATIONSHIP WITH GOD is not a fleeting, passing acquaintance. It is a lasting, abiding friendship. He has promised us: "I will never fail you nor forsake you" (Heb 13:5). "Lo, I am with you always, to the close of the age" (Mt 28:20). "My sheep hear my voice, and I know them, and they follow me; and I give them eternal life, and they shall never perish, and no one shall snatch them out of my hand" (Jn 10:27-28). Here is the basis then on which we can "pray without ceasing."

God has pledged himself to us in steadfast love and fidelity. He will never leave us. He is always near to us, always at our side. He exercises an unswerving initiative on our behalf.

So scripture exhorts us, "Pray at all times in the Spirit, with all prayer and supplication," Paul tells us in Ephesians 6:18. And again, in 1 Thessalonians 5:17, "Pray without ceasing." These are expressions of a constant, continual, never-ending relationship; an ongoing adventure on our part of sharing with the Lord the hopes and aspirations of our lives. Just as he will never leave us, so he asks us never to leave him out.

But what does it mean to pray "without ceasing"? This is not an injunction to join a monastic order, or spend all our time on our knees. Rather, it is an invitation to redirect our restless, energetic minds, which never lie dormant, into positive streams of communication with God, concerning all that is going on around us as well as within us.

We never stop thinking. Have you ever been in a large city during the rush hour, when thousands of people pour out of office buildings and shops and factories, and stream home in endless cascades of automobiles, buses and trolleys and trains? All those people, all those minds working ceaselessly and frantically.

And what are they thinking about? To what is all that brain power being given? Has it ever crossed your mind that most of that energy is being negatively expressed? It is extraordinary the amount of energy we put into worrying and anger. We brood over insults. We chide ourselves for mistakes. We lament opportunities missed. We belittle our superiors. We are threatened by those we are supposed to lead. We go through imaginary conversations as we prepare our response to someone who irritates us "just one more time."

And Christians fall into the same trap. It is so easy. The natural human sinful disposition is to "scratch the mortar out of someone else's wall." What a waste of energy!

When scripture encourages us to pray without ceasing, and to cast all our care upon him, it is literally saying redirect those restless, energetic minds into a positive stream of communication with God. Turn it all into prayer! Instead of nursing our wounds and self-pity, pray for the grace to forgive. Instead of worrying about those for whom we are responsible, ask God to intervene and lift the burden from our shoulders. Instead of thinking creatively about how to bring someone else down, pray creatively about how to build them up.

When I lived in England, my landlady had a little wall plaque that read, "Why pray when you can worry?" I always saw the humor of it, and the reverse psychology was good for me. It always drove me to really say, "Why worry when you can pray?"

Part of the marvelous freedom we enjoy as God's children is that we can talk to him at any time, about anything. The point of "Pray without ceasing" is not that we *must*, but that we *may*. When we lie down at night, we can talk with God. When we rise in the morning we can talk with him. We can talk to God when we brush our teeth (after all, what else is there to do then?). We can talk to him as we drive in our car. Many of us are already in the habit of talking under our breath to the other drivers anyway. Why not talk to God instead?

Similarly, when you think of someone, pray for them. It may be a son who needs a job. It may be a mother recovering from illness, a daughter struggling with peer pressure. Have you ever noticed that most of your "thinking time" is about people and not things? What a powerful influence for good we Christians can be if we pray for those people.

Just to give you one more illustration, what about the people who are in the public eye? What about the newscaster on your favorite station, the star in your favorite TV program, the president of the United States, the crisis upon crisis that our news stations love to bring to us? We are always thinking, therefore someone nearly always has our attention: pray for them.

"But this is fanaticism!" you say. "Who wants to pray all the time? Are we never to think of anything besides God?"

Of course there are times when we must think of other things, times when we must give our undivided attention to the issues at hand. But we need to do so *as in the presence of God*, against the backdrop of a constant relationship and his constant love. We don't talk to him every single moment. But we do walk in the Spirit, aware of a constant relationship, knowing that the Lord is present with us as we get on with the business at hand.

Our relationship with the Lord, like all relationships, goes through different times and seasons. Take, for example, the relationship between husband and wife. There are times of intense intimacy, of almost overpowering affection. We sometimes wish these would go on forever, but they don't. They ebb and flow, now rising, now subsiding into what we might call a more undramatic workaday relationship. It is the same in our day to day living with God. There are times of basking in the sunshine of his love on the high plateaus, and times of just moving on through the less exciting terrain which makes up much of our common human experience. But just as husband and wife live out their lives against the backdrop of being married, so do we live out the entirety of our lives against the backdrop of a constant relationship with God. He is always there, always loving us, always ready to listen to us. As we recognize his unwavering commitment to us, we are able to live in the day to day adventure and challenge of his presence. We enjoy the dialogue. It's as if we say, "Oh, I must talk to him about this!"

One last insight. Our minds never do rest, they are always at work, always thinking, so that even when we sleep there is a continual unconscious cerebration—a processing, compiling, sifting, sorting, reworking. If all the data being unconsciously processed has been previously prayed over, then an extraordinary phenomenon takes place. God goes to work in those unconscious recesses of our mind. Even while we are asleep, prayers are having their effect and God is preparing the answers and responses that will seemingly "pop into our heads" out of nowhere.

> *Lord, make us aware of your nearness to us. Help us to turn our minds and hearts to you more freely and completely. Transform the perfunctory details and routines of life into times of prayer and sharing with you.*

For reflection and discussion:

—Do I restrict my relationship with God to specified times and places, or do I go about my day in constant communication with him?

—What are some perfunctory elements of my daily routine that I can turn into opportunities for fellowship with God?

SIXTEEN

Boldness in Prayer

Let us then with confidence draw near to the throne of grace.
(Heb 4:16)

"THE WORD OF THE LORD CAME to Jeremiah a second time, while he was still shut up in the court of the guard: 'Thus says the Lord who made the earth, the Lord who formed it to establish it—the Lord is his name: Call to me and I will answer you, and will tell you great and hidden things which you have not known'" (Jer 33:2-3).

Call to me and I will answer you. This is the amazing invitation the Lord gives, not just to Jeremiah but to all of us who are his children. He wants us to come into his presence. He wants us to pray to him. He wants to open his heart and mind to us, and to tell us *great and hidden things which you have not known.* So he invites us in.

Think about that for a moment. The Lord of all the universe desires our company, and so *he* invites *us* to come into his presence. Our prayer, then, is a response to God's invitation.

Of course it is we who need him, not he who needs us. It would be logical to expect that we would have to ask to be allowed in. If necessary, we would be willing to beg and plead to come before him.

It is entirely appropriate that we should have these feelings.

After all, he is the magnificent Creator and we are the dependent creatures; he is the King of kings and we are the subjects. There is a certain audacity in our claiming the right to come before him. It is rather like a beggar on the streets of London coming to Buckingham Palace with a crust of bread and asking to be allowed to give it to Queen Elizabeth.

A couple of years ago, during a sabbatical leave, I took my family back to England for a visit. As part of our touring, we visited the place in Gloucester where Prince Charles and Princess Diana live. The thought flitted across my mind, wouldn't it be fun to meet them? Wouldn't it be nice if my little daughter Sarah could spend the afternoon with their little son, Prince William? After all, they are the same age.

Well, we did get to the gates of the estate. We have a nice photograph of our Sarah, perched on my back, holding onto the splendid gates across the driveway. But of course we never got in. Standing there, I realized what a colossal piece of audacity it would be to expect admission; I felt a bit awkward even thinking about it.

There came a time in King David's life when he realized the same thing. At the end of his life, after having commissioned his son Solomon to reign after him, he called upon the people to contribute their riches toward the building of the temple. They responded with overwhelming generosity.

But when the time came to present the offering to the Lord, David was overcome with the awareness of God's greatness, and of his own smallness and the insignificance of this national gift before God:

> Therefore David blessed the Lord in the presence of all the assembly; and David said, "Blessed are thou, O Lord, the God of Israel our father, for ever and ever. Thine, O Lord, is the greatness, and the power, and the glory, and the victory, and the majesty; for all that is in the heavens and in the earth is thine; thine is the kingdom, O Lord, and thou

art exalted as head above all. Both riches and honor come from thee, and thou rulest over all. In thy hand are power and might; and in thy hand it is to make great and to give strength to all. And now we thank thee, our God, and praise thy glorious name.

"But who am I, and what is my people, that we should be able thus to offer willingly? For all things come from thee, and of thy own have we given thee." (1 Chr 29:10-14)

Who are we, indeed, that we may come into God's courts? Yet the wonder of prayer is that God requests the audience. We could not come unless he did. If we were the least bit aware of who God is and who we are, we *would not* come if he did not invite us. But he does. He does not make us beg and plead; he takes the initiative and invites us in.

"Let us then with confidence draw near to the throne of grace, that we may receive mercy and grace to help in time of need" (Heb 4:16). In the King James version, this verse reads, "Let us come boldly before his throne of grace." I like that word *boldly*. Because God has issued us the invitation, we have the privilege—in a certain sense, the right—to come boldly into his courts.

Sometimes when we pray we can feel like God's poor relations, who have been admitted to his banquet but don't really quite belong there. We feel unsure of ourselves, as though at any moment someone were going to notice us and say, "What are *you* doing here?" But we aren't interlopers who have sneaked in the side door. We are invited guests; we have been summoned to the banquet by the host himself; we *belong* there. Therefore, let us come boldly before his throne of grace.

Lord, were it not for your gracious invitation we would not dare to approach your throne. But you have invited us, and so we draw near to you with confidence. Help us to appreciate the great privilege you give us by inviting us into your courts.

For reflection and discussion:

—How thoroughly do I understand that my prayer is a response to God's invitation, that he desires to spend time with me?

—What obstacles prevent me from responding to God's invitation?

SEVENTEEN

An Open Ear

This is my beloved Son; listen to him. (Mk 9:7)

ONCE WHEN I WAS SPEAKING on prayer as a relationship, I was really challenged by a young man in the audience who came up to me after the session and asked, very respectfully but very pointedly, "Doesn't a relationship imply listening to God as well as speaking to him?"

He was right, of course. In my talk that day I had fallen into the same trap that so many of us fall into when we pray: seeing prayer as a one-way communication, with us doing all the talking and God doing all the listening.

What an impoverished relationship that would be! We know from our human experience that a successful relationship cannot work on that basis. We all recognize, of course, that one of the keys to being a good friend is being "a good listener." But a relationship becomes one-sided if one party does all the talking and the other party does nothing but listen.

This is just as true in our relationship with God as in any other. If, in our mind, "praying" simply means us talking to God, we are missing the most important part of prayer. God is more than willing to listen to us, but he wants to speak to us as well.

The psalmist thanked God for having given him "an open ear" (Ps 40:6). We too must approach our times of prayer with an open ear, ready to hear God speak to us.

How do we listen to God in prayer? How does he speak to us?

Most obviously, he speaks to us through his word in the scriptures. The books of the Bible are, as someone has said, "love letters from our heavenly homeland." They are God's most direct and certain communication with us. "For whatever was written in former days was written for our instruction, that by steadfastness and by the encouragement of the scriptures we might have hope" (Rom 15:4). We are robbing ourselves of God's expressed desires for our lives if we neglect to make scripture reading and study a regular element of our prayer. "All scripture is inspired by God and profitable for teaching, for reproof, for correction, and for training in righteousness, that the man of God may be complete, equipped for every good work" (2 Tm 3:16).

Sometimes God communicates internally to us by speaking to our heart or to our spirit—our inner sense of "knowing." Most of us have this experience at one time or another. A particular thought or impression forms in our minds and somehow we know that it is not a fleeting fancy, but the Holy Spirit who has planted it there. It may be a prompting to take some particular action, or to say something to a particular person. It may simply be a renewed awareness of some truth that we already know in our minds but that has not yet sunk into our hearts. Often during the course of our regular scripture reading, a passage we have read dozens of times before will suddenly leap out at us and grab our attention, and we know it is the Lord speaking to us through that passage in a personal way.

Sometimes God actually speaks to people in an audible voice, or at least speaks "to the heart" so forcefully that they cannot really tell afterward whether they heard an audible voice or not. My own brother is one such person.

Tony is a successful businessman in England. He brought his family over to the States for a visit a few years back. He was not a Christian except in the vague cultural sense in which virtually all Englishmen consider themselves Christian. While he was here we had the opportunity to talk about Jesus and the difference he could make in Tony's life. Before he left, my wife and I gave him a copy of J.B. Phillips' translation of the New Testament.

For a while after Tony got back to England, his thoughts about Jesus got shelved amid the pressures of his job, his family, moving to a new house, and so on. The New Testament we had given him also got shelved.

Then one Sunday after church, for some reason Tony got a sudden impulse to read that New Testament. "Where's that book John and Kathie gave us?" he asked Chris, his wife. "You know, that book by Phillips." (It is, perhaps, a measure of his religious training and spiritual condition that he didn't call it "The Bible" or even "the New Testament" but "that book by Phillips.") She remembered where it was and got it for him and he sat down and began to read.

He skimmed through chapter 1 of Matthew, the genealogy of Jesus, and then settled into the narrative telling of his birth and early ministry. He was midway through the Sermon on the Mount (chapters 5-7) when he heard a voice say, "Jesus is my Son, you know."

Who had said it? His children were playing quietly in the next room; not them. His wife was in the kitchen preparing lunch; not her. He looked to see if they had even heard the voice. They hadn't! He went upstairs and, like any good little English boy, knelt down by the side of his bed to pray. He had a profound sense of the Lord's presence. As he knelt there, his whole life flashed before his eyes and he began to weep for the years he had wasted; suddenly he *knew* that Jesus was God's Son, and everything he had done apart from Jesus suddenly seemed so meaningless.

Had he really heard anything? To this day he is not absolutely sure. But he does know that, audibly or not, God *spoke* to him; his life has not been the same since.

I must immediately tell you that I have never heard the Lord speak audibly to me and, while most of us would love it, it is only on very rare occasions he chooses to do it. But God will speak to us, too, if we will take the time to listen to him. In the ninth chapter of Mark's Gospel we read the account of Jesus' transfiguration. Peter, James, and John have accompanied Jesus up the mountain; they have seen him gloriously trans-figured before their eyes; they have seen him speaking with Moses and Elijah. Suddenly, "a cloud overshadowed them, and a voice came out of the cloud, 'This is my beloved Son; *listen to him.*' And suddenly looking around they no longer saw any one with them but Jesus only" (Mk 9:7-8).

What God said that day to Peter, James, and John he also says to us: Jesus is my Son. *Listen to him.*

Important to growing in our ability to discern God's voice are certain practical guide lines.

1. *Keep notes*, whether of thoughts that come from your Bible reading or impressions made upon your heart as you pray. Then pray about those "leadings" and ask God to show you whether they are from him.

2. *Test by the standard of scripture* anything you suspect is God's 'nudge' in your life. He will never lead you to disobey his revealed truth in scripture (2 Tm 3:16).

3. *Obey known and explicit commands from God's word.* I have known people who count themselves deeply spiritual, and as such are only interested in "exotic" spiritual leadings and ignore the common "garden" variety. This is a fake spirituality. God leads in the secret places of the heart those who follow him in the open places of his commands from scripture.

4. *Weigh by the counsels of the godly.* Every serious Christian should be part of a fellowship group. We are not going to mature as Christians unless we spend quality time with Christian friends in which vulnerability and trust are devel-oped. It is in the company of such a group of fellow believers that we can test God's call to us. They know us well, and can pray with us as we seek to discern God speaking.

Father, give us an open ear and help us quiet ourselves before you, that we might hear you speak to us in prayer. Open our hearts to receive your word as it comes to us in scripture and in the quiet of our hearts.

For reflection and discussion:

—Are my times of prayer characterized more by talking to God than by listening to him? How can I remind myself to listen to God when I pray?

—What are some of the ways God speaks to me? How can I learn to avail myself of them more faithfully?

EIGHTEEN

Humbleness
Leads to Prayer

Everyone who exalts himself will be humbled,
but he who humbles himself will be exalted. (Lk 18:14)

WE HAVE SPOKEN of our creatureliness before God, of the audacity it would take for us to presume to come into his presence were it not for the fact that he invites us to come in. All this speaks of the need for us to humble ourselves when we pray. Jesus had something important to say on this subject.

Two men went up into the temple to pray, one a Pharisee and the other a tax collector. The Pharisee stood and prayed thus with himself, "God, I thank thee that I am not like other men, extortioners, unjust, adulterers, or even like this tax collector. I fast twice a week, I give tithes of all that I get." But the tax collector, standing far off, would not even lift his eyes to heaven, but beat his breast, saying, "God, be merciful to me a sinner!" I tell you, this man went down to his house justified rather than the other; for everyone who exalts himself will be humbled, but he who humbles himself will be exalted. (Lk 18:10-14)

Let us be clear at the outset that this is not a threat. If you say to your child, "Don't put your hand into the fire or you'll get burned," is that a threat? Are you saying, "If you put your hand

97

there I'm going to come over and burn you"? Of course not. You are simply explaining the way things are. Fire is hot; if you put your hand in it, you get burned. That's not a threat, that's a law of nature.

In just the same way, Jesus in this parable is making a statement of fact, not a threat. He is not saying, "Look, you had better humble yourself, folks, or—pow!—I'm going to knock you down a few pegs myself." He is simply explaining a principle that God has built into human life, a "law of spiritual nature" if you will. If we, according to the spirit of our age and the tendencies of our fallen human nature, seek to exalt ourselves, the natural repercussion built into things by God is that we will be humbled. Pride brings us down.

We have been trained to be self-sufficient. Almost from day one, our secular environment has taught us not to become dependent on others but to make our own way, to chart our own course, to construct our own set of values—to create, if it were possible, our own world. Where does prayer fit into such a life? What possible meaning can it have for us? If we are masters of our fate, to whom are we to pray?

But it is no use. We cannot be our own God. All we succeed at doing is "exalting ourselves," glorifying the fantasy image we have of ourselves and our capabilities, deluding ourselves into thinking we are in control of our destiny, until the day when all our plans and dreams and delusions come crashing down around us.

How many times do we see this pattern repeated? How many marriages have collapsed, how many families fallen apart, how many lives been ruined, because we put our selves and our plans and our methods ahead of God and God's plans and God's methods? The only possible outcome of such an ego orientation is our undoing. He who exalts himself shall, inevitably, be brought low.

Ah, but then he shall learn the truth about himself, and about God, and then he shall pray! When all our delusions of success and grandeur have crumbled, then we are driven to the place where we come before God on our knees. And in that humility we can pray. In that humility we can receive the grace of God and be exalted by his glory.

If we continue to follow our own path, the natural order of things is that a humbling awaits us. But we *can* spare ourselves the painful experience of being humbled by the consequences of our own self-centeredness. We *can* humble ourselves, bring our life as it is and surrender it to Jesus Christ, and in due course we will be exalted as his grace works in us and his plan for our life is brought about. This is not merely a one-time decision we make, this surrender, this humbling; it is a decision we make each day. Whether it comes through circumstances or by our own choice, humbleness leads to prayer.

If my people who are called by my name humble themselves, and pray and seek my face, and turn from their wicked ways, then I will hear from heaven, and will forgive their sin and heal their land. (2 Chr 7:14)

Lord, teach us the true meaning of humility. Help us to humble ourselves, to surrender our lives to you, that we may experience your grace and power working in us. Teach us the humbleness that leads us into communion with you.

For reflection and discussion:

—What are some areas in my life in which I am following my own course instead of surrendering to God's will?

—How can I learn to humble myself daily and so enter more fully into the privilege of prayer?

Part IV

The Practice of Prayer

NINETEEN

Alone with God

He rose and went out to a lonely place, and there he prayed.
(Mk 1:35)

ONE OF THE MOST STRIKING aspects of Jesus' public life was precisely that it *was* so public. Everywhere we turn in the gospels, we find Jesus surrounded by crowds, followed by crowds, literally *hounded* by crowds of people.

It is no wonder this was the case. Wherever Jesus was, there was truth, there was healing, there was deliverance, there was caring. The people—there seemed no end of them—who needed to hear the truth, and who needed healing and deliverance, who needed to know that someone cared about them in this hard impersonal world, were drawn to him as to a magnet. He was the greatest popular sensation of his day.

The pressures on him must have been enormous—all the more so because he had no choice but to live, as we say, in a fishbowl. Unlike the famous people of our day, who are able to seclude themselves in the elegant isolation of their mansions and estates, Jesus had "nowhere to lay his head" (Mt 8:20). He was always in the open, always within reach, always "on display."

And so his insistence on praying in solitude is all the more noteworthy. From the very beginning of Mark's Gospel we see him in action, recruiting a corps of disciples, teaching, preaching, healing, casting out demons—and then, "in the morning, a great while before day, he rose and went out to a lonely place, and there he prayed" (Mk 1:35). Even then, his disciples "pursued him, and they found him and said to him, 'Everyone is searching for you'" (1:36-37). But the pattern has been established. Jesus' ministry will henceforth be marked by periods of intense public activity, punctuated by times of solitude for reflection and prayer.

These times of solitude were not just intermittent escapes, a last resort taken when the pressures became too intense. They were a regular, habitual feature of Jesus' life. At one point, Jesus heals a leper and tries to get the man to keep quiet about his healing. Jesus probably knows it won't work, and it doesn't: "But so much more the report went abroad concerning him; and great multitudes gathered to hear and to be healed of their infirmities. But he withdrew to the wilderness and prayed" (Lk 5:15-16).

But he withdrew. The New American Standard version translates this phrase, "But he himself would often slip away." It carries the sense of something planned, a habit carefully developed and maintained. In the midst of all the busyness, Jesus made it a point regularly to get away and be alone with his Father.

Hudson Taylor, the great missionary to China, used to bemoan the many demands on his time and say, "The busier I am, the more I need to get away and pray." How different we are! We are more apt to say, "I'm so busy, I just can't get away and pray," and let it go at that.

Solitude is a lost ingredient in modern life. We seem, in fact, to go out of our way to fill our lives, from morning to night, with all manner of noise and clamor. We have clock radios to wake us up and car radios to keep us company and telephones to keep us within reach at any hour of the day. We have agendas and "to-do lists" and pocket schedule books to help us impose order on the chaos we engineer for ourselves. We are never quiet, never at rest, never alone.

But if we are to be men and women of prayer, we must take our cue from Jesus, who carved out times of solitude in the midst of his hectic life. It was in those times that he found the refreshment he needed to go back into action.

There are, of course, other settings for prayer than personal solitude. There are the times we gather with the congregation for corporate worship, just as Jesus attended synagogue weekly. There are times for prayer in the family or in small groups of fellow believers, just as Jesus prayed regularly with his disciples. But there must also be time to be alone with God.

It won't just happen; we will have to make it happen. Jesus had to take definite steps to gain and preserve his times of solitude. He sometimes had to rise unusually early; so may we. He sometimes had to stay up late into the night; so may we. On at least one occasion he had to dismiss the crowds and order his disciples to go on ahead without him (see Mk 6:45-46); we may sometimes need to overrule the demands of associates, friends, even family, to make time for solitary prayer. Jesus apparently found it worth the effort, and worth the risk of appearing "stand-offish," to be alone with his Father in heaven. So must we.

Solitude has become so alien to us that the prospect can seem cold and barren. But Jesus clearly relished being alone with God. To him, it was not merely a "spiritual discipline" or a "religious duty." It was a joy, a delight. Jesus knew who he was as the beloved Son of God, and he loved to spend time alone with his Father.

We, too, are the beloved children of God; may we likewise come to take delight in times of prayer alone with God! Read Psalm 37:4 in the context of prayer: "Take delight in the Lord, and he will give you the desires of your heart."

Heavenly Father, we pray that you will help us recognize our need to be alone with you in the midst of our busy lives. Help us take the necessary steps to make times of solitude and reflection a regular part of our life.

For reflection and discussion:

—Do I regularly set aside times to be alone with God in the course of my life?

—What steps will I need to take to make such times a reality?

TWENTY

No Pain, No Gain

For the moment all discipline seems painful rather than pleasant.
(Heb 12:11)

I AM SORRY TO HAVE TO BRING UP a subject that I know will seem unappetizing. But I am afraid I have no choice. I could hardly write a book intended to help you with your prayer life if I did not speak to you about the importance of discipline.

"Discipline" has become a dirty word in our culture. For older folks it suggests school days, sitting under the glare of a stern teacher, fearful of getting our knuckles rapped if we make the slightest misstep. Or it suggests the army, regimentation, being under a compulsory schedule of activities from dawn to dark, mindlessly "following the program."

Surely we have left all that behind! This is the age of spontaneity, of freedom. Discipline is a hang-up—necessary for children, perhaps, but not for us. We are grown-ups now, we can handle our affairs without subjecting ourselves to anything so distasteful as (shudder) *discipline*.

I know I am speaking heresy in many circles, but spontaneity is greatly overvalued. The "spontaneous" person who shrugs off the need for discipline is like the farmer who went out to gather the eggs. As he walked across the farmyard toward the hen house, he noticed the pump was leaking. So he stopped to fix it. It needed a new washer, so he set off to the barn to get one. But on the way he saw that the hayloft needed straightening, so he went to fetch the pitchfork. Hanging next to the pitchfork was a broom with a broken handle. "I must

make a note to myself to buy a new broom handle the next time
I get into town," he thought, and headed for the kitchen to jot
it down. When he opened the kitchen door, the hinge
squeaked loudly, so he . . .

By now it is clear the farmer is not going to get his eggs
gathered, nor is he likely to accomplish anything else he sets
out to do. He is utterly, gloriously spontaneous, but he is
hardly free. He is, if anything, a prisoner to his unbridled
spontaneity.

The fact of the matter is that discipline is the only way to
freedom; it is the necessary context for spontaneity.

Christians sometimes say, for example, that they don't want
to use a "canned" approach to sharing the gospel. They want to
be "free" to be "led by the spirit." Then when an opportunity to
witness arises, they are tongue-tied. Their desire for "freedom"
has bound them up; they are not free to pursue the opportunity the Lord has given them.

The person who has not learned to add and subtract is not
free to balance his checkbook. The musician who has not
practiced his scales and chords if not free to learn a new song.
Discipline is the key to freedom. This is as much the case with
prayer as with any other activity.

When I say we must be disciplined in our prayer life, I do not
mean we must be rigid or mechanical. I simply mean we must
construct a framework for prayer, inside which we and the
Holy Spirit can move about freely. There are number of
elements to such a framework.

First, we must simply *decide that we are going to pray,* every
day, come what may. There are times when prayer is effortless
and enjoyable, and we find it easy to be faithful to it. But there
are also times when, if we left it to our feelings of the moment,
we would just as soon take a day (or a week) off. Prayer must
rise above the "good intention" stage and become a firm
resolution of the will. This is the foundation upon which our
framework will be built.

Second, we should decide to *pray for a specific period of time.*

Fifteen minutes might be enough at first. Later, as we grow in the ways of prayer, we will want to pray longer. There is, of course, nothing to prevent us from exceeding our specified period when inspiration prompts and circumstances allow. But we need a solid base from which to start.

Third, it is helpful to *pick a particular time to pray.* "First thing in the morning" seems best for most people, though some find other times—lunch hour, before dinner, before bedtime—more suitable. When we leave prayer to be "squeezed in somewhere," it frequently gets squeezed out.

It is also helpful to *pick a special place to pray,* where we will be free of distractions and able to turn our attention fully to the Lord.

Finally, it is good to *have at least a general plan for how we will spend our time in prayer.* This need not be too rigorous; simply deciding ahead of time that we will, for example, begin with a psalm, read two chapters of scripture (one Old Testament and one New Testament) and meditate on them briefly, pray for a list of people and situations we have written down, and close with the Lord's Prayer, helps us avoid the quandary of coming to prayer time and then having to figure out "what to do next."

A further recommendation which will get you well organized is a daily Bible study guide and devotional journal called *My Time with God.* (It can be obtained from the National Institute of Christian Leadership, P.O. Box 300, Sewickley, PA 15143.)The Bible study guide will help you with systematic daily scripture reading. It provides a brief explanation of the passage and questions to help sharpen your understanding.

The accompanying *My Time with God* devotional journal will help you with your note taking and prayer times. There are even photo album-style pages in the journal so that you can place pictures of people for whom you are praying and not just lists of names.

None of these "disciplines" are intended to box us in. Quite the contrary! They are intended to set us free. As time goes on we should feel free to modify them to suit our changing needs.

Developing our prayer life is not unlike an athlete developing his abilities. "Every athlete exercises self-control in all things," Paul observes (1 Cor 9:25). Athletes pursue rigorous disciplines in order to grow stronger, faster, more agile. They have a saying that sums it up: "No pain, no gain." Without the pain of self-discipline, there can be no progress. This, too, holds true in spiritual matters: "For the moment all discipline seems painful rather than pleasant; later it yields the peaceful fruit of righteousness to those who have been trained by it" (Heb 12:11).

The disciplines I have recommended in this chapter are not terribly rigorous. But they are important. I can confidently assure you that once you have built them into your prayer life, you will never want to be without them.

Lord, help us to embrace discipline in prayer as a key to growth in our life with you. Teach us to order our lives so that we may ensure adequate and fruitful time to be with you.

For reflection and prayer:

—Do I avoid discipline in a way that robs me of the freedom to grow in my prayer life?

—Have I taken time to construct an adequate "framework" within which I can be free to pray as the Spirit leads?

TWENTY-ONE

The Eye of Faith

I saw the Lord sitting upon a throne. (Is 6:1)

I WOULD VENTURE TO SAY that without the use of the imagination in prayer there can be very little communication that is meaningful—at least to us.

Prayer in its simplest terms is a conversation with God. As with any conversation there is someone there listening to us. I have had numerous inquiries, especially by new believers, on how to talk to the Lord when you can't see him. That question leads us immediately to how we imagine God when we speak to him.

The imagination is our ability to create mental representations of reality—to see things in our mind's eye. Amongst the many varied ways in which we use our imagination, faith and prayer, two very interrelated subjects, are both crucially dependent upon the imagination.

For instance, faith and imagination are inseparably linked. Without imagination how does one exercise faith? To quote the scripture on the issue, "Now faith is the assurance of things hoped for, the conviction of things not seen" (Heb 11:1). We can also render this, the "realizing"—the "making real"—of things not seen. This proper use of the imagination is one way of making the unseen things of God more real to us, and thereby experience them by faith.

So it is with prayer. Let us look at three common forms of prayer and consider how our imagination can help us with each.

First, there is our corporate worship—the prayer we engage in when we gather in church on Sunday morning, for example. How do we imagine God when we join together in a hymn or in corporate prayer?

I like to picture the Lord enthroned in glory, seated at the head of the assembly. This is how Isaiah described him: "I saw the Lord sitting upon a throne, high and lifted up; and his train filled the temple" (Is 6:1).

I likewise envision us, his people, gathered together before his throne, praising and worshiping him, acclaiming his glory, like so many subjects of a great king gathered in his courts for a special audience. This is how John portrayed the worship that goes on unceasingly in heaven: "I looked, and behold, a great multitude which no man could number, from every nation, from all tribes and peoples and tongues, standing before the throne and before the Lamb, clothed in white robes, with palm branches in their hands, and crying out with a loud voice, 'Salvation belongs to our God who sits upon the throne, and to the Lamb!'" (Rv 7:9-10). I sometimes even see us joined to that great congregation in heaven right now, and join my worship to that of dear Christian friends who have already gone on to be with the Lord Jesus.

What about our times of private prayer, our daily devotions? Some of us struggle with how to imagine God when we do not have the familiar "props" of church pews and organ music and stained-glass windows.

Let me suggest that as you kneel to pray, you picture the Lord Jesus standing before you. You are kneeling at his feet. You see the scars from the nails in his feet and are reminded of the love he showed in dying for you on the cross. You see his hands reaching out to embrace you. You see his face. Perhaps as you recall and repent of your sins you see him looking at you and loving you as much as the day he died for you.

In your imagination you bring other people to the Lord in prayer, set them before him and ask him to be at work in their lives. Or you see the Lord going to them: walking into the hospital room of someone who is sick; visiting the home of friends in distant cities; dropping by your husband's office or your son's classroom. As they go about their daily occupations, you see the Lord Jesus with them. Those whom you want to come to know the Lord as Savior, you see yourself bringing to him, your arm around their shoulder introducing them to him.

As a young Christian I asked a minister friend what he did with his mind when he prayed. He said he saw himself kneeling before and looking into a bright and glowing lighted presence, not giving it a form, but knowing that it was the Lord of glory to whom he was speaking. While I have found it more helpful to see the Lord "right there," ever since then I have loved the sunlight shining on me, especially in a place like a restaurant. In my imagination, I see the Lord shining down on me in all his love and power, warming my heart toward him, and making my face glow with his presence.

This brings me to another kind of personal prayer where our imagination can help us. I call it "prayer on the run." We know that we need not confine our time with the Lord just to our daily devotions. The Lord is with us all day long. When you drive to work or to the store, picture the Lord sitting with you in the car as you converse with him. See him there with you in the office as you pray about your calendar and your work projects; there with you around the house as you cook and clean and do the laundry.

"Prayer on the run" is the experience of knowing that "in him we live and move and have our being" (Acts 17:28).

It is by this creative and positive use of the imagination that we learn to bring to the Lord all the little things that make up our lives. The way we deal with these little, everyday things will determine how we deal with the larger, more difficult circumstances that come our way. When we have not shared the common everyday places and experiences, we feel awkward coming to him with the big things, as if we were taking advantage of God, as if we didn't belong.

"Prayer on the run" is living with the Lord in the little events so that when the crises occur, prayer is not a "panic move" (it's come to that, has it?) but a natural extension of the way we live our workaday lives. "Prayer on the run" means "peace instead of panic" when calamity and disaster intrude. "Prayer on the run" is "looking to Jesus, the author and finisher of our faith" (Heb 12:2 KJV).

Let me close by inviting you to apply your imagination to that first resurrection morning.

Imagine you are there. Imagine your home, right now, is the setting. "As they were saying this, Jesus himself stood among them" (Lk 24:36). Because the Lord Jesus is alive, for you to use your imagination to see Jesus standing right next to you right now is not sheer fantasy. See him by faith.

Now imagine that he is talking to you. "Why are you troubled, and why do these questionings rise in your hearts?" (Lk 24:38).

Use your God-given imagination not just to *see* the Lord Jesus, but also to hear him ask you about your doubts and fears. He knows them. Refusing to admit them won't hide them from him. Remember, he is the one "unto whom all hearts are open, and all desires known." But the way he speaks to you is not a cruel accusation. Somehow hearing him ask you about those "questionings" has a way of causing them to evaporate. He asks you in love and compassion.

Now feel his touch. "It is I myself, handle me and see" (Lk 24:39). As by faith you *see* the Lord Jesus, and as by faith you *hear* the Lord Jesus, so now by faith reach out and *touch* him. Know that as you reach out to him, he reaches out to you. Even as you move to embrace him, he embraces you.

Now count yourself among those to whom Jesus says, "My sheep hear my voice, and I know them, and they follow me; and

I give them eternal life, and they shall never perish, and no one shall snatch them from my hand" (Jn 10:27, 28).

See! Hear! Touch! Believe!

Father in heaven, thank you for our imaginations. Forgive us that we so often use them wrongly, and help us to use them rightly. Help us to see you in our mind's eye as we come together to worship and as we come before you in personal prayer.

For reflection and discussion:

—Do I feel comfortable with the idea of using my imagination in prayer?

—How do I picture God in my mind's eye when I pray? How can I use my imagination to make his presence more real to me?

Part V

Overcoming Doubt
in Prayer

TWENTY-TWO

Doubt, Disobedience, and Doublemindedness

He who doubts is like a wave of the sea that is driven and tossed by the wind. (Jas 1:6)

THE ENGLISH HISTORIAN, Sir Arthur Bryant, described the ineffectiveness of a particular political leader in the days before World War II in these words: "There is nothing more destructive of action than a tortured, undecided mind."

Few of us have escaped the agony that comes from facing a difficult choice while being "in two minds," trying to reconcile two incompatible values or beliefs, or courses of action. Some people go through life with a whole raft of such incompatible convictions, never resolving the tension, forever hung up on the horns of one dilemma after another.

This is especially true with regard to our spiritual lives, including prayer. There is nothing more destructive to the action of prayer than a mind tortured by doubt. Yet it is the common human experience. We come into God's presence, and at once our minds are clouded by unresolved questions, uncertainties, anxieties. Our relationship with God is impaired, our confidence in prayer destroyed.

Make no mistake, doubt is the great destroyer of prayer. "For he who doubts is like a wave of the sea that is driven and tossed by the wind. For that person must not suppose that a double-minded man, unstable in all his ways, will receive anything from the Lord"(Jas 1:6-8).

This is all the more sad when we consider what a privilege it is to pray. God, the living Lord, the sovereign ruler of all creation, invites us into his presence. Us! You and me! What a wonder! As the psalmist says, "When I look at thy heavens, the work of thy fingers, the moon and the stars which thou hast established; what is man that thou art mindful of him, or the son of man that thou dost care for him?" (Ps 8:3-4). What a tragedy for us to lose this privilege, to be robbed of it by doublemindedness and doubt!

All of us are plagued by doubt from time to time, but some of us know it as virtually a constant companion. But know this: God wants to set us free from doubt and restore us to confidence and freedom in his presence. In the remaining chapters we will consider some of the doubts which undermine our prayer life, and how we can overcome them.

The number one cause of doubt and doublemindedness is *wrongdoing*. Doubt always follows hot on the heels of sin.

Why? Because an act of wrongdoing is an attempt to live in two kingdoms at once. As Christians, we live in the kingdom of light. But when we sin—when we know we have done wrong and do not repent, when we know we are doing wrong and do not stop, when we know we are about to do wrong and do not alter our course—we are consciously planting one foot in the kingdom of darkness.

This is just as true with sins of omission as it is with sins of commission. We all know that when we do something God has forbidden, it is sin: the sin of *commission*, of actively going against God's will. But when we *fail*, or *refuse*, to do something God *has* commanded, that too is sin: the sin of *omission*, of omitting to do what God has willed.

"Whoever knows what is right to do and fails to do it, for him it is sin" (Jas 4:17). Our knowledge of "what is right to do" comes primarily from scripture. God has made his ways and will clear. There are also those unmistakable "taps on the shoulder" which the Holy Spirit gives us from time to time. Either way, when we do not do what we know to be right, for us it is sin.

The immediate by-product of sin is doublemindedness. We have planted our feet in two kingdoms at once. We are trying to live in two worlds, trying to serve two masters at the same time. We limp along between what we are and what we are supposed to be. The fruit of this doublemindedness is doubt. How *can* we come confidently before God in one arena—prayer—when we know we have backed away from him in another arena—practice?

If the first cause of doubt is wrongdoing, then the first remedy for doubt is *repentance*. Isaiah makes clear both the debilitating effects of sin and the mercy of God toward repentance:

> When you spread forth your hands,
>   I will hide my eyes from you;
> even though you make many prayers, I will not listen;
>   your hands are full of blood.
> Wash yourselves; make yourselves clean;
>   remove the evil of your doings from before my eyes;
> cease to do evil, learn to do good;
> seek justice, correct oppression;
> defend the fatherless, plead for the widow.
> Come now, let us reason together, says the Lord:
> though your sins are like scarlet,
>   they shall be as white as snow;
> though they are red like crimson,
>   they shall become like wool. (Is 1:15-18)

Furthermore, "If we say we have no sin, we deceive ourselves, and the truth is not in us" (1 Jn 1:8). If you find your prayer plagued by doubt and doublemindedness, be honest with God: come to him and confess your sin. Take inventory of the things in your life you know to be wrong; ask God's forgiveness for them and call upon him for the power and persistence to set them right. Because "if we confess our sin, he is faithful and just, and will forgive our sins and cleanse us from all unrighteousness" (1 Jn 1:9).

Through the death and resurrection of our Savior, Jesus Christ, the guilt of all our sins can be wiped away. Let us run to his cross and avail ourselves of the mercy and forgiveness he offers us!

Lord, even as you have made known to us by your Spirit the sins and failings that hinder our fellowship with you, give us by that same Spirit the grace to seek forgiveness. Renew our ways, that we may come to you, not in the confusion of a double mind, but in the confidence of a single mind.

For reflection and discussion:

—Am I aware of areas of wrongdoing in my life that weaken my relationship with God and hinder my prayer?

—What concrete steps can I take to repent of my wrongdoing and receive the grace of forgiveness?

TWENTY-THREE

Walk in the Light

God is light and in him is no darkness at all. (1 Jn 1:5)

THERE IS YET MORE to be said about the role of guilt in causing us to experience doubt in prayer. In the last chapter we discussed what we might call the objective fact of guilt: we *are actually* guilty because we have disobeyed God. In this chapter we will look at the subjective feeling of guilt, the personal sense of dirtiness or unworthiness, that plagues us when we come to present ourselves before the Lord in prayer.

Obviously, the two are not unrelated. One of the reasons we may *feel* guilty is precisely because we *are* guilty: we have done wrong; we know we have done wrong; and our conscience is continually reminding us that we have done wrong.

But sometimes what we experience is not so obviously related to any known, identifiable act of wrongdoing. We just *feel* dirty and uncomfortable in God's presence. We feel unworthy, as though we had no right to be there. When we question the very appropriateness of coming before God, we automatically find our ability to communicate with him strained.

Now, it is not hard to understand why we might feel dirty or impure in the presence of God: in comparison with his absolute holiness and purity, we could hardly feel otherwise. "This is the message we have heard from him and proclaim to

you, that God is light and in him is no darkness at all" (1 Jn
1:5).

Sometimes, in an effort to minimize our sense of unworthiness, we try to minimize God, to bring him down to our level.
If we cannot measure up to the standard, why then, let us
change the standard! "God won't mind *that* much. After all,
I'm doing pretty well. I'm not such a bad sort. He won't notice
a few little sins here and there." But it is no use. God is who he
is; we cannot reduce him or diminish him. We must let God be
God and acknowledge our sin to be sin.

When Isaiah encountered God, he found himself in the
presence of one who was, "Holy, holy, holy" (Is 6:3). Isaiah's
immediate response was absolutely appropriate: "Woe is me!
For I am lost; for I am a man of unclean lips" (6:5). God is
light, pure and radiant and utterly unadulterated; in him there
is no darkness, "no variation or shadow due to change" (Jas
1:17). His holiness is the standard against which we are
measured. So a healthy appreciation of who God is rightly
gives us a healthy sense of unworthiness in his presence.

But the problem we are talking about is not a healthy
awareness of our sinfulness as we come into the presence of a
holy God; it is rather a destructive sense of filthiness and
unworthiness which comes from hiding in the shadows away
from God.

Read carefully: "If we say we have fellowship with him while
we walk in darkness, we lie and do not live according to the
truth; but if we walk in the light, as he is in the light, we have
fellowship with one another, and the blood of Jesus his Son
cleanses us from all sin" (1 Jn 1:6-7). There is a kind of
hiddenness, furtiveness, that ruins our fellowship with God.
The apostle John calls it "walking in darkness." The antidote is
obvious: we must instead walk "in the light," come out into the
open. It is only then that "the blood of Jesus his Son cleanses us
from all sin."

One of the most important things we can do to enhance our
relationship with God is to come out into the open with him,

into the light. We must walk, not in the twilight of the shady side of the street, but in the open sunlight of his shining face.

Many of us are used to thinking of our faith as a "private" affair, something intensely personal. And so it is, in an important sense; because of the uniqueness of each of us, there are aspects of our relationship with God that we could never articulate to anyone. But that is not the same as having a hidden, secretive faith.

One of the tragedies of our modern culture is the way we shut ourselves off from one another. We are afraid and mistrustful of other people, even those close to us. We are afraid they will reject us if they find out what we are really like. So we hide behind a carefully constructed facade and live an isolated, timid, "safe" existence.

The problem comes when we begin to relate to God from behind that same facade, as though he did not already know what we are like and might think badly of us if he did. But of course he already does know us, and loves us anyway. It is only our mistaken sense of privacy that holds us back.

We need to step out into the light, to let God beam the sunshine of his love on the whole of our personality. We need to throw open the closets and let him come in, let him show us who we really are and what we can really be with him.

Above all, we need to let him show us how thoroughly he loves us, how completely his blood washes away the filthiness of our sin. Obviously we are not going to come out into the open with God if we think he is going to mercilessly crush us once we get there! But no, he calls us into the light, not to embarrass us or punish us, but so that we can be thoroughly cleansed by his forgiveness.

When we walk in the light, we come to the open ground of the cross where Jesus died for us. There we are vested with all the righteousness and beauty of Jesus himself. Let us walk in the light, as he is in the light, that we might have fellowship with him and that the blood of Jesus might wash away all our sin!

Lord, as we come before your cross help us to experience being washed clean in the blood of the Lamb. In our own strength it is impossible, but by your power we can come and be made new. Help us to open up the dark places in our lives to the light of your love, and the joy of your forgiveness.

For reflection and discussion:

—Do I have the confidence in God's love for me that would enable me to come full out into the open with him?

—What are some areas I have tried to keep hidden from the Lord, giving rise to a sense of unworthiness in his presence?

TWENTY-FOUR

Ignorance Is Not Bliss

Behold, I have graven you on the palms of my hands. (Is 49:16)

ONE OF THE MOST COMMON reasons we experience doubt when we come before the Lord in prayer is that we do not grasp his magnificent promises to us. Perhaps we simply do not know them, have never heard them. Perhaps we are superficially familiar with them but have never grasped them and made them our own. Or worst of all, perhaps we *have* heard them, but have chosen to ignore them, to act as though God had made no such commitments to us.

God has made breathtaking promises to us throughout the scriptures. They can provide for us a firm anchor of security in the midst of our turbulent times and stormy lives. But if we do not *know* these promises, and really own them in the depths of our personality, we cheat ourselves of their power. We become very uncertain as to whether God cares about us, let alone whether he hears us when we pray to him. This is one area where ignorance most assuredly is not bliss.

Let us look briefly at two of God's most incredible promises to us; promises which, once we have genuinely made them our own, can dispel our doubt and substantiate our faith.

But Zion said, "The Lord has forsaken me,
my Lord has forgotten me."

> "Can a woman forget her sucking child,
> that she should have no compassion
> on the son of her womb?"

Even these may forget, yet I will not forget you.

Behold, I have graven you on the palms of my hands.
(Is 49:14-16)

"The Lord has forsaken me, my Lord has forgotten me." This, of course, is where so many of us begin: we feel God has totally lost sight of us, if indeed he ever knew of us in the first place.

We may feel this way simply because we see ourselves as so small, so insignificant, so undeserving of God's love. Or it may be that current circumstances are getting us down. Perhaps we have lost a job, or been bypassed for a promotion; perhaps our marriage is in difficulty or our health poor. Whatever the reason, we feel God has abandoned us. Some even reach a point where merely seeing other people experiencing joy and success in the Lord rankles them, and their despair deepens.

Obviously, if we feel forsaken or forgotten by God we are not going to feel much assurance in praying to him.

But the Lord reasons with us: "Can a woman forget her sucking child, that she should have no compassion on the son of her womb?"

The presumed answer is, of course not. And the Lord says, "Even these may forget, yet I will not forget you." As strong as the devotion of a mother is to her child, stronger still is God's devotion to us.

He underlines his unswerving faithfulness: "Behold, I have graven you on the palms of my hands." It was a Jewish custom, when a son or daughter was away from home, to inscribe their name on the palm of your hand, so that as you went about your work during the day, you would be constantly reminded of them. God says he has done the same with us: our names are "graven" on the palms of his hands, always before him, never to be erased.

Are we ready to believe this first promise? That God knows every Christian believer by name? That he has graven us on the palm of his hand? That he will never forget us, never forsake us? That we are dearer to him than the child suckled at the breast of its mother?

Thou dost keep him in perfect peace,
  whose mind is stayed on thee,
  because he trusts in thee,

Trust in the Lord for ever,
  for the Lord God
  is an everlasting rock. (Is 26:3-4)

A woman once told me the tragic story of how she had lost her little girl. The family had been on vacation, staying in a motel, and the eleven-year-old daughter climbed out of the outdoor swimming pool and ran to her room at the poolside. A live electric cable ran from the room to a radio at the poolside; the motel door had been closed on the cable and cut through the insulation. When the little girl took hold of the door handle she was electrocuted.

An experience like that would be more than enough to send most of us into serious depression, to say nothing of anger with God. And yet, this woman told me, she and her husband had experienced a quiet peace throughout the ordeal. Why? Because they kept their mind stayed, or fixed, upon Jesus. He kept them in perfect peace because they trusted in him. As she told me the story, she pressed into my hand a piece of paper on which was written Isaiah 26:3-4, "Thou dost keep him in perfect peace, whose mind is stayed on thee." It was that truth which had seen her through her tragic loss.

Fortunately, few of us are confronted by pain and loss of this magnitude. But sadly, we still manage to lose our peace for significantly lesser reasons. Our minds are hyperkinetic, always flying from one thing to another. Our personalities are fragmented, now playing one role, now another. We seldom experience the inner peace for which we long.

Where is it to be found? Not in attempts to organize ourselves into a trouble-free peaceful environment. No matter how organized and "on top of things" we get, at the office or around the house, true peace simply does not lie there. Nor is it within our selves. Despite the grand promises of all the modern self-help pop-psychology books, we simply do not have within ourselves the avenue to true peace.

The promise of scripture is that *God* will keep us in *perfect* peace as we choose to fix our minds and hearts upon him. Again, we must embrace this truth, make it our own, and apply it consciously to our lives. A deliberate, self-conscious act of the will must be made to center our lives around Jesus.

There are many other passages in scripture that speak to us of God's intimate and personal care and faithfulness toward us. I have cited two famous examples. Perhaps you already know of other such promises that God has used in the past to speak to you. Make those promises your own. Learn them by heart—not just by memory, but *by heart*. Believe them. Act upon them. Draw upon them. When doubt begins to assail you as you come before the Lord in prayer, claim those promises and choose to believe them.

Lord, help our weakness where we have failed to grasp your word to us. Forgive our sin where we have heard it but ignored it. Remind us that we are graven upon your hands. Help us to keep our minds stayed upon you that we may experience perfect peace in the midst of conflict. By the power of your Spirit, Lord Jesus, convince us who know you that you hold us close to your heart.

For reflection and discussion:

—Do I doubt God's love and concern for me? How can I lay hold of the truth of his word that he will never fail me nor forsake me?

—What are some other scriptural promises I can learn to remind me of God's faithfulness and my privileged access to him?

TWENTY-FIVE

Jesus Understands Suffering

Because he himself has suffered and been tempted, he is able to help those who are tempted. (Heb 2:18)

C.S. LEWIS SAID that one of the reasons he had stubbornly remained an atheist for so long before his conversion to Christ was what he called "the problem of pain." Why was there pain and suffering in the world? He could not reconcile their existence with the so called God of love, and so refused to believe in that God for many years.

We who already are convinced Christians can find ourselves disturbed by this same problem, though in a different form. In our case, it does not lead us to call God's existence into question. Rather, it erodes our confidence in his love, and causes us to be extremely doubtful and even bitter when we come to God in prayer.

We are all too familiar with the many different forms that human pain and suffering take: physical, psychological, emotional, relational, even spiritual. We have experienced it in our own lives. We have watched it prey upon others.

The world, it seems, is filled to overflowing with pain and suffering of one kind or another. The closer to home it comes the more keenly we feel it, and the more we empathize with C.S. Lewis' complaint. Why *is* there so much suffering? Our inability to come to grips with this problem can erode our confidence in God and undermine our prayer.

The scripture points us to five main reasons why there is suffering in the world.

First, there is suffering in the world because of the Fall. When Adam and Eve chose to disobey God, to go their own way rather than his way, they in effect rejected the life of excellence and joy he had planned for them and opted for a life of pain and separation from God. Their sin—which we call original sin—opened the door to death, to distortion of the human personality, to pain and suffering. Because we are all part of the human race we all suffer this human dilemma (see Rom 5:12).

Second, there is suffering because of sin—not only original sin, but also specific sins that we and others commit. No sooner have we seen human nature corrupted by Adam and Eve than we see Cain murdering his brother, Abel. Both of them suffered from it. Abel lost his life, and Cain had to live forever after with the guilt pangs and repercussions of his evil deed (see Gn 4:8-14). All of us have known suffering because of sins we have committed and because of sins others have committed against us.

Third, there is suffering because of the work of Satan. We live in the midst of a spiritual battleground. Certainly Jesus made this clear through his own ministry, which included not only healing but also the casting out of the demonic. Some Christians are scandalized by the very notion of the existence of evil spiritual forces and refuse to believe in them; others are obsessed by the idea and "see demons behind every bush." We must, on the one hand, come to terms with the biblical truth that "your adversary the devil prowls around like a roaring lion, seeking someone to devour" (1 Pt 5:8). On the other hand, we must not be intimidated and phobic about the world of spiritual evil. The Lord defeated Satan and his legions at Calvary. But much of the suffering we see in the world is because the cross of Christ has been rejected, and Satan has taken full advantage.

Fourth, there is suffering for righteousness' sake. Jesus promised that those who followed him would experience trials and persecutions on his account. He also promised that such suffering would bring a deep sense of happiness (Mt 5:10-11) and was to be welcomed rather than evaded.

Finally, suffering sometimes comes because of misfortune or accident. Things "just happen;" pain comes our way "due to circumstances beyond our control." This is actually just a subset of the sufferings we experience because of the Fall, but it is worth noting separately because its very nonrationality is part of its painfulness.

We now have a clearer picture—clearer, perhaps, than we would have liked—of what suffering is about and from whence it comes. But still the temptation comes to blame God. In the face of that temptation, let me suggest these conclusions from the teaching of scripture.

1) Suffering is not God's original plan for us, but occurs because of the fallenness of life in our world. God is not up in heaven "zapping" us with sickness and pain, any more than he is causing us to sin. He hates both sin and suffering, and will ultimately deliver us from both.

2) Suffering is not given in order to teach us, though through it we may learn. God does not send afflictions to "teach us a lesson." He does, however, enable us to learn from the afflictions that come to us.

3) Similarly, suffering is not given to us in order to teach others, though through one another's suffering we may learn.

4) Suffering does not occur because of our weak faith, though through it our faith may be strengthened. Many a person's faith has been shipwrecked because of faulty teaching that suggests that if their faith were strong enough they would never suffer.

5) God does not depend on human suffering to achieve his

purposes, though through suffering his purposes are sometimes achieved. The one exception to this was the Lord Jesus, whose suffering and death accomplished our redemption (2 Cor 5:18-21).

6)Suffering is not always to be avoided at all costs, but is sometimes to be embraced. It is better to suffer for righteousness' sake than to sacrifice righteousness to avoid suffering.

7)Suffering can tear us down or build us up, depending on our response. We can let it make us either *bitter* or *better*.

Perhaps the most important thing to keep in mind is that Jesus understands suffering, both our suffering and that of the whole world. He himself bore that suffering, in his own body, as he hung upon the cross. And because he himself has suffered, he is able to help us with our sufferings as well (see Heb 2:18). His promise to us is sure: "Come to me, all you who labor and are heavy laden, and I will give you rest" (Mt 11:28).

> *Lord, we come to you with hearts and minds and bodies filled with suffering, surrounded by a world of pain. Lift us up by the power of your cross and resurrection and enable us to come to you for peace in the midst of pain and sorrow.*

For reflection and discussion:

—Am I able to trust in God's power and love despite the problem of pain in the world around me?

—Are there particular pains or sufferings in my own life that weigh me down in prayer? How can I call upon the Lord's help to rise above them?

TWENTY-SIX

An Everlasting Memorial

Remember the wonderful works that he has done. (1 Chr 16:12)

THE STORY IS TOLD of two men—let's call them Harry and Stan—who have known each other for some time. Harry has fallen upon hard times and has come to his old friend asking for help.

"Why come to me?" Stan asks. "Why should I help you out? What have you ever done for me?"

"What have I ever *done* for you?" Harry gasps. "Why, don't you remember when your house burned down several years ago and you and your family moved in with me?"

"Yes, I remember. But . . ."

"And what about the time your child was in danger of drowning and I jumped into the lake to rescue him?"

"Yes, but . . ."

"And how about the time you lost your job and I gave you all that money? Don't you remember? I've done lots for you through the years!"

"Everything you say is true enough," Stan says. *"But what have you done for me lately?"*

How similar we are in our relationship with God! We are such ungrateful people. Over the years God has been at work in our lives and families, bringing us to himself, restoring us and watching over us, providing for us—and so many times we come to him complaining, "But God, what have you done for me lately?"

It is striking how many times throughout the Old Testament God insisted that his people establish some form of memorial to him and to his deeds on their behalf. For God is a God who acts, a God who intervenes in the affairs of humanity, a God who reaches from eternity into time and makes himself known by his actions. It is God's intention that by remembering and pondering his deeds, we refresh our memory as to what he is like and cultivate our relationship with him.

All this has great relevance to our prayer life. One of the reasons we experience doubt in prayer is that we get all caught up in the pressures and pains of the moment, and we forget what God has done for us in the past. Obviously, then, one of the best ways for us to overcome doubt in prayer is to actively call to our remembrance the good things God has done for us.

King David taught this lesson to the Israelites. When he had finally ascended to his throne, David had the ark of the covenant brought up to Jerusalem for a celebration. When all the people had gathered together before the Lord, David led them in a psalm of thanksgiving:

Remember the wonderful works that he has done,
the wonders he wrought, the judgments he uttered.
O offspring of Abraham his servant,
sons of Jacob, his chosen ones! (1 Chr 16:12)

David knew how prone to forgetfulness his people were, and how important it would be for them always to remember the great things God had done for them. When the Israelites forgot God's deeds on their behalf, they strayed from him and got into trouble. It is the same with us.

What does it mean, practically speaking, for us to remember God's faithfulness?

When we are sick and tempted to doubt God's presence because of our illness, we can remember the times when we were well, when God blessed us with strength and vigor. We take our health for granted—until sickness comes; then we grumble and complain about it. We need to call to mind, in the middle of the bad times, the good times God has given us in the past and can give us again in the future.

We can call to mind God's continuing provision for our life. Moment by moment we are held in his care. Day by day we are given life and food and shelter and safety, all from God's hand.

We can remember the particular things God has done for us in answer to our prayers. One of the simple reasons we forget what God has done for us is that we don't keep a record of it! Many Christians keep a notebook in which they write down the requests they make of God, the date they first prayed for them, and the date on which God answered their prayers. It is amazing how quickly we can compile our very own "book of chronicles" of God's goodness in our lives. Then, when in prayer we are tempted to doubt, we can reach for our notebook and remind ourselves of what the Lord has done for us.

Finally, we can create our own "memorials" to God's special actions of grace in our lives. For me, one such memorial is the dining room at a youth ranch where I first met the woman who became my wife. We have gone back there on vacation to see it, and have made a point of showing it to our children: it is still there, the very table at which we sat that evening. Even when I am not there to see it in person, I can see it in my mind's eye, an "everlasting memorial" to one of God's greatest gifts to me.

Whatever form it takes, we need a fixed chronicle in our minds of the good things God has done for us, so that when we are tempted to believe God is no longer involved in our life, we can turn our attention to our memorials of his care and concern for us, and encourage ourselves as we pray to him.

Father, we thank you for your great faithfulness to us. Help us to remember that faithfulness when we are tempted to doubt it.

Defend us from despair by reminding us how good you have been to us in the past, and give us confidence that you will again act on our behalf in the present and the future.

For reflection and discussion:

—Do I fall prey to the "What have you done for me lately?" syndrome in my relationship with the Lord?

—What are some of the most notable things God has done in my life, which I can recall as an "everlasting memorial" of his faithfulness?

TWENTY-SEVEN

Risking All

Seek first his kingdom. (Mt 6:33)

EVERY FRIDAY I LEAVE my church in the suburbs and drive to downtown Pittsburgh, where I preach at a lunch-hour gathering for working people called "Thank God It's Friday." And every Friday several hundred men and women leave their shops and offices and walk or drive to Trinity Cathedral to worship together and to listen to me teach. That time together is very important. For many of those who attend regularly, it represents a spiritual oasis in the midst of a secular desert. Some have expressed that time to be an escape from the kingdom of Mammon for a brief celebration in the kingdom of God.

And yet there is something about that perspective that betrays a mistaken understanding of the Christian life, and that points to one of the reasons why we are often beset by doubt when we try to pray.

It is simply this: we are trying to live in two kingdoms at once. Monday through Friday we live in the kingdom of job and career, except for Friday lunch hour when we step across the line into the kingdom of God. For many of us, it is a more comprehensive problem. We are living, twenty-four hours a day, seven days a week, fifty-two weeks a year, in a kingdom built by ourselves and ruled over by ourselves. Isn't that often the case? We are trying to be the ruler of our own little world, with occasional forays onto God's "turf."

But it doesn't work that way. There is no place for divided loyalty with Jesus. Small wonder that during our brief visits to his kingdom we feel unsure of our ground, uncertain of our status.

Jesus' classic teaching on this subject is found in the Sermon on the Mount, where he teaches us to place every aspect of our lives—even our relatively mundane needs, like food and clothing—under his Lordship. It climaxes with a verse that is very familiar to us: "Seek first his kingdom and his righteousness, and all these things shall be yours as well" (Mt 6:33).

Perhaps the impact of this teaching has been lost upon us, precisely because of the familiarity of the passage and the pleasant little tunes to which we have grown accustomed to singing it. Jesus is telling us to get off the throne. He is telling us we cannot live in two kingdoms—his and ours—at the same time. We must come all the way over into *his* kingdom.

This feels like risky business. If there is one thing most of us do not want to give up, it is our control over our lives, plans, careers, families, and futures. The thought of turning it all over to the leadership and lordship of Jesus is a bit frightening. We're not sure we want to go that far out on the limb. And yet the Lord's word to us is that the *only* way to maximum fulfillment and security lies in maximum surrender, maximum risk-taking for his sake (see Mt 16:25).

This is all well and good as a spiritual principle. But what might it mean for us in concrete terms? Let me mention three ways God calls us to "lay it on the line" for him and for his kingdom.

The first is sharing our faith with others. It is strange, but I know Christians who can walk up to a perfect stranger and try to sell him something and not be intimidated in the least. They're salesmen. That's how they make their living. But when it comes to sharing the gospel, however, even with a friend or relative, they are petrified! Why? Because we have the idea that sharing our faith with another person jeopardizes our relationship with them. We are afraid they will reject us. And one thing our "kingdom" cannot face is the prospect of having its king—us—cut off at the knees and rejected.

Now, I suspect we have less to fear than we think—we are not going to find ourselves nearly as mocked and despised for sharing the gospel as we fear we might be. And yet if risking some of our relationships, and some of our self-protectiveness, is what it takes to seek first God's kingdom, then it is a risk we must take.

A second area has to do with our material possessions, our money, our homes, our "estates." I have known people willing to put up everything they own as collateral for a financial investment—and I have known people who have lost everything doing so. Are we willing to "lay it on the line" for the kingdom of God, for God's work, in the same way? How much of our effort is invested in building up our own estates, our own capital, and how much is invested in expanding the kingdom of God? Perhaps we are afraid God will ask us to become a pauper for his sake. Statistically speaking, that is not terribly likely. God does not call very many people to that way of life. But it is a risk we dare not avoid taking. For where our treasure is, there will our heart be also.

The last area is our time and energy. Once when I was playing golf on vacation, I happened to meet a man who had worked as a golf pro at a local country club. But he had left that job, he said, in order simply to play golf full time. "I want to find out just how good I can get," he told me. Now there is commitment! That man was willing to lay *all* his time and *all* his energy on the line—for the sake of *golf*! Are we willing to do the same for the sake of Christ? God might not call us to drop everything and chart a radically different course with our life. Then again, in some way and to some degree, he just might. It is a risk we shall have to take.

The question is simple, really. Whose kingdom are we seeking first? Ours or God's? We know we cannot expect peace and joy putting our own kingdom first. But neither can we try to live in two kingdoms at once. We cannot know confidence in God's presence until we are willing to stake everything on his kingdom, until we take the risk of coming all the way in.

Lord, we acknowledge that we have not sought you and your kingdom above all things. Create new hearts in us, and give us the courage to risk what we have and who we are for your sake and the gospel's. Make us powerful in prayer because we have lived powerfully for you.

For reflection and discussion:

—Do I find myself seeking my own kingdom ahead of God's kingdom, trying to live in two worlds at once?

—Are there ways in which God is calling me right now to risk my relationships, my possessions, my time and energy, for the sake of his kingdom? How can I respond to him?

Yes, No, Wait, Grow

Father, I thank thee that thou hast heard me. (Jn 11:41)

IF I WERE TO ASK YOU the main reason you sometimes feel bothered by doubt when you pray, you would most likely answer, "Because I have prayed before and God has not answered my prayer. How can I have confidence he will hear me this time?" I know that is the most likely answer because I have asked the question many times, of many people, and that is the answer I most frequently hear.

It is easy to see why unanswered prayer would cause us such difficulty. If indeed God has not heard us when we have prayed in the past, then why pray to him now? If, as it appears, he has not answered previous requests we have made of him, then why assume he will answer this time? How are we to overcome the doubt that unanswered prayer raises in our minds?

The fact is that there is no such thing as unheard or unanswered prayer. God *always* hears us when we pray to him, and he *always* answers our prayers. Does this sound impossible? Yet he has promised us that is shall be so. We have seen him promise Jeremiah, "Call to me and I will answer you" (Jer 33:3), and that promise holds for us as well. We see Jesus, before he calls Lazarus out of the tomb, saying, "Father, I thank thee that thou hast heard me. I knew that thou hearest me always, but I have said this on account of the people standing by, that they may believe that thou didst send me" (Jn 11:41-42). Just as the Father never failed to hear and answer Jesus his Son, so he never fails to hear and answer you and me, his sons and daughters.

If we are to come to grips with this, we must first clarify what we mean when we talk about "prayer."

To pray means far more than simply to make requests of God. Throughout this book, we have been at pains to see that prayer is more than going to God with our shopping list of needs and desires. Rather, it is the expression of a deep and intimate relationship, in which we open our hearts and minds to God, and he to us. If our sole experience of prayer has been to present God with a continually updated list of "non-negotiable demands," then to stand back and expect him to respond to our requests upon demand and *in the precise manner* we demand, then our entire attitude and approach toward God is hopelessly awry.

Some of us have become quite practiced in this form of prayer. We have even spiritualized it. We ask for what we want, then tack on the magic words, "in Jesus' name," as a sort of magical incantation that assures the desired results. Or we find someone to "agree" with us regarding our request, hold our Bible up and call God's attention to Matthew 18:19 ("If two of you agree on earth about anything they ask, it will be done for them by my Father in heaven"), and command him to produce what we have asked for.

But who is the sovereign and who the servant? Is it God who is answerable to us, or we to him? To pray "in the name of Jesus" means to pray according to the will and character of Jesus, not simply to tack a phrase onto the end of a request. And to reach the point where we "agree with" one another means to let ourselves be shaped and molded *into* conformity with the will and character of Jesus by our mutual teaching and correction.

One of the most wonderful answers to prayer that I personally have been a part of took place in the Pittsburgh Eye and Ear Hospital. One of my church members, Loren Cockrell, was in for eye surgery.

At the end of a busy day I drove through Pittsburgh and into the marvelous medical complex attached to the University of Pittsburgh and made up of an array of teaching hospitals. I parked the car and made my way up through the Eye and Ear Hospital, to Loren's room. The door was ajar, and all was dark inside.

Here is how Loren described what happened before the congregation some time later.

I was in the Eye and Ear Hospital three days before John visited me. I had been operated on for a detached retina. At that time, I was 99 ½ percent blind in my left eye. I had been told that with the operation, I would probably regain 25 percent of my vision. Three days after the operation, the surgeon decided that the operation was a failure and I would have to have more surgery. With the second operation, if successful, I would have less than 25 percent vision. That was not a happy thought but I had no alternative. I had to submit to the operation. I was certainly in great distress the night before surgery. The lights were out in the room, the door opened and there was John Guest.

I was very happy to see him. John sat by my bed, held my hand and prayed a healing prayer. He left and I was at peace for the first time that day.

For some reason my thoughts turned to a passage in the Bible that I had read long ago, the tenth chapter of the Gospel of Saint Mark, beginning at the forty-sixth verse. Jesus was leaving Jericho and along the road were many people gathered to see him. Among them was a blind man named Bartimaeus, and he called out as Jesus passed, "Jesus, Son of David, have mercy on me!" Jesus said, "What do you want me to do for you?" And the blind man said, "Master, let me receive my sight." His sight was restored and Jesus said, "Go your way; your faith has made you well."

I was relaxed and went to sleep. The next day I was rolled into the operating room, hooked up to the intravenous feeding and knew that within a very short time, the Pentothal would be turned on. Within a second or so I would be asleep. I knew something had to be done quickly, because I knew I had been healed.

I asked that the doctor be brought in. They told me he could not be disturbed because he was scrubbing up, preparing for the operation. And I said, "Well, get him and don't let me go to sleep!" The doctor came in and asked what I wanted. He was annoyed. Probably it was the first time anything like this had happened. I said, "Doctor, I think a change has taken place in my eye. I think I have been healed. Will you look at it?" He did and said, "By damn, you're right!"

The people in the operating room were in turmoil. They had never seen anything like this happen before. They said, "How did it happen?" I said, "John Guest did it." Those were the exact words I said. "Who is John Guest?" they asked. I told them to come to St. Stephen's some Sunday and find out. I told John about this later and he said, "I didn't do it, it was done by the Lord." Regardless of who did it, I feel that the Holy Spirit was truly at work that night. The next day I walked out of the hospital and I had my sight. As of a check-up a month ago, I have 20/20 vision in my left eye.

When Loren made the announcement about his 20/20 vision, the congregation burst into applause, very much in awe of what the Lord had done in this quiet-spoken and reserved gentleman.

Obviously, the Lord had given his yes to the prayers offered for Loren, but in my sermon later in the service I raised the question, "What if the Lord's answer had been no—would you the congregation have burst out in applause?" I asked, "What if Loren had *not* been healed, but the Lord's grace *had* been sufficient for him to deal with his partial blindness—would there have been thanksgiving to God?"

Sometimes God's answer is no. Look at 2 Corinthians 12:7-9:

> And to keep me from being too elated by the abundance of revelations, a thorn was given me in the flesh, a messenger of Satan, to harass me, to keep me from being too elated. Three times I besought the Lord about this, that it should leave me; but he said to me, "My grace is sufficient for you, for my power is made perfect in weakness." I will all the more gladly boast of my weaknesses, that the power of Christ may rest upon me.

Irrespective of how some try to massage away the implications of Paul's words, it is plain that the Lord said in effect, "No, Paul. Not your way, but mine." And the great apostle, through whom God had done so many wonderful things, "gladly boasted" in whatever it was that brought weakness or infirmity, because by it the "power of Christ" rested upon him. Sometimes, we have to face it that the Lord says no.

Remember that prayer occurs in the context of our relationship with a father who loves us. Now, many of you are parents yourselves, and you know perfectly well that you do not grant every request made of you by your children. They are less wise, less experienced, less discerning than you; sometimes they ask for things that would do them harm. So you answer them, and the answer is no. That is the most loving answer you could give them. They may not understand or appreciate that fact, but it is true nonetheless.

Obviously, it is the same with us and our Father in heaven. God is more concerned about our long-term sanctification than about our short-term satisfaction. We make many requests that from his perspective are clearly dangerous or harmful to us. So he answers us, and the answer is no. He has some better plan for us. We may not understand or appreciate it, but when God says no, it is a loving answer.

Obviously, we are happiest when he answers yes. But we should be just as appreciative when he answers no. It is just as much a sign of his love for us. It does not mean he has not heard us; it means we have asked for something outside his will, something he knows we will be better off without.

But what about those times when we feel sure—because of a clear teaching of scripture—that our prayer *is* valid, *is* within his will? We have prayed for the salvation of a friend and we know it is God's desire for "all men to be saved and to come to the knowledge of the truth" (1 Tm 2:4), and they have not yet come to faith in Christ. What then?

There is a third answer God may give us. He may answer yes, he may answer no, and he may answer, "Wait." All things must happen within the context of God's overall plan, in the manner and at the time that are suitable in his eyes, not ours. Perhaps God has not yet purified our motives. Perhaps he is seeking to strengthen our character by calling us to persevere in prayer. Perhaps he has unfinished business remaining with the person for whom or situation for which we are praying. Perhaps there are other factors at work of which we simply can have no idea.

Ultimately, our confidence in prayer rests in God's steadfast love. We trust his knowledge of what is best for us. We do not presume that, like a doting parent, he will accede to our every whim. God does hear all our prayers. And he does answer them, every one of them. Yes, no, wait, grow. Each is an appropriate answer, designed for our benefit.

Here is a little saying that sums it all up: When the *idea* is not right, God says "no." When the *time* is not right, God says, "slow." When *we* are not right, God says, "grow." But when everything is right, God says, "go."

Lord, help us to grow in love for you and in trust of your care and concern for us. Teach us to pray "in your name," according to your character, and to rejoice in the answer you give us—yes, no, wait, grow—as a sign of your fatherly love for us.

For reflection and discussion:

—Have I let my confidence in prayer be shaken by past answers of "no," "wait," or "grow"?

—How can I learn to pray more purely according to the will and character of Jesus?